Photoshop Magic:

Expert Edition

D0863074

Photoshop Magic:

Expert Edition

BY BRENDON PERKINS

Hayden
Books

Photoshop Magic: Expert Edition

Library of Congress Catalog Number: 96-72156
ISBN: 1-56830-416-1

Copyright © 1998 Hayden Books

Printed in the United States of America 1 2 3 4 5 6 7 8 9 0

Warning and Disclaimer

Trademark Acknowledgments

President	Richard Swadley
Publisher	John Pierce
Managing Editor	Lisa Wilson
Director of Marketing	Kelli S. Spencer
Product Marketing Manager	Kim Margolius
Director of Software and User Services	Cheryl Willoughby

The Photoshop Magic Team

Acquisitions Editor
Jawahara Saidullah

Development Editor
Beth Millett

Copy/Production Editor
Michael Brumitt

Technical Editor
Bill Vernon

Technical Edit Coordinator
Lorraine E. Schaffer

Publishing Coordinator
Karen Williams

Marketing Coordinator
Linda B. Beckwith

Cover and Book Designer
Gary Adair

Manufacturing Coordinator
Brook Farling

Production Team Supervisor
Brad Chinn

Production Team
Michael Henry
Linda Knose
Tim Osborn
Staci Somers
Mark Walchle

Indexer
Christine Nelsen

Composed in Bembo and Gill Sans

Hayden Books

The staff of Hayden Books is committed to bringing you the best computer books. What our readers think of Hayden is important to our ability to serve our customers. If you have any comments, no matter how great or how small, we'd appreciate your taking the time to send us a note.

You can reach Hayden Books at the following:

Hayden Books
201 West 103rd Street
Indianapolis, IN 46290
317-581-3833

Internet: hayden@hayden.com
Visit the Hayden Books Web site at http://www.hayden.com

About the Author

Photoshop Magic: Expert Edition is **Brendon Perkins**'s first book, but he is not new to the graphics scene. He often writes for *3D Design Magazine* and has provided Photoshop images that have appeared on the covers of several graphics publications. Brendon holds a Bachelor of Science degree in Mechanical Engineering, which he received from GMI Engineering & Management Institute located in his home town of Flint, Michigan. He currently lives in the shadows of the monuments in our nation's capitol where he works as an aerospace engineer. During his free time, Brendon often dabbles with Photoshop and other computer–based graphics tools, but he also gets out into the sun occasionally to enjoy the sights of the mid-Atlantic region and beyond.

Acknowledgements

I'd like to thank my roommate, Tom, for his support and assistance with the numerous, daily chores that needed to get done during the development of this book. I'd also like to thank my little sister, Michelle, who has always encouraged me to continue on to bigger and better things while she also shares unconditionally in the excitement of each new project that I undertake. Now she's got a good reason to use that new computer that she just bought. I'd also like to thank the numerous friends who have provided encouragement and continually looked after my welfare during the past several months. Finally, I'd like to thank Beth, Jawahara, Michael, and Bill, as well as the rest of the staff at Hayden Books for making the development process go as smoothly as it did.

Dedication

This book is dedicated to my parents without whom none of this would have been possible.

Contents at a Glance

Contents

x

Introduction

This text is designed to go beyond the basics to provide 12 specific techniques for producing professional looking graphics using Photoshop 4.0. Whether you're interested in producing graphics for the web, developing special effects, or retouching old photographs, this book shows you how to unleash the power of Photoshop and take full advantage of the application's extensive tool set. Each of the 12 techniques guides you through the specific, individual operations that are required to complete the sample images.

If you're an advanced user of Photoshop, you'll find the step-by-step structure of each technique easy to follow, so that you can complete the sample images efficiently without having to weed through a lot of excessive information. Nevertheless, the book is supplemented with numerous sidebars filled with suggestions, tips, tricks, and other useful information about Photoshop to help you learn more about the application as you go. But that's not all. Even though the techniques make use of numerous, advanced capabilities and concepts, they are written in a straightforward, explicit manner, so that even beginners can implement them without much prior experience with the application. This book also provides you with a Basics chapter that is referenced throughout the individual techniques with blue, highlighted text, so that you can look up additional information as needed.

Although this book can serve as a tutorial for Photoshop users who like to learn by way of example, I anticipate that many readers will find this publication to be useful as a reference for completing more advanced tasks. I also hope that you find the techniques and sample images to be useful as sources of inspiration to develop ideas of your own. As I'm sure you'll agree, Photoshop is a powerful application that goes a long way to help you unlock your own hidden talents, but it's definitely no substitute for inspiration, and good examples are often hard to come by. In this sense, it is my intent to help fill the void with the content of this book, and I hope that you enjoy it.

When it comes to the production of digital imagery, there is no doubt that artistic talent must be balanced with a great deal of technical knowledge to ensure quality and consistency in your work. In fact, I suspect that it's common for many new users of Photoshop to familiarize themselves with the user interface, only to discover that the real power of the application requires some knowledge of the underlying mathematics of manipulating bitmapped images. Until recently, I used to think that my artistic and technical skills were completely unrelated and would remain so, but like many producers of computer-based art, I've discovered that it is precisely these two skills areas that enable computer-based artists to eventually master such applications as Adobe Photoshop.

Photoshop is also a sophisticated program and it's not always obvious which combination of operations is required to produce a specific outcome. As a result, it can often take quite some time for new users to develop prescribed methods of dealing with common circumstances without having to spend countless hours of experimentation to find the right sequence of steps—not to mention the individual settings—that are required to complete a specific task. Nevertheless, you can learn from the previous experience of others, and picking up this book is a positive step in that direction. This book provides you with everything you need—except Photoshop itself—to complete the sample images that are presented. Whether you follow the techniques literally or experiment to produce variant images that suit your own specific needs, I'm sure you'll learn something new, and you'll have fun while doing it.

Photoshop 4.0

All of the techniques of this book were completed with Photoshop 4.0, which is the version that I recommend you use. If you're attempting to duplicate these techniques using an earlier version of Photoshop, you will not have all the capabilities required to complete all of the techniques exactly as written. Furthermore, your results may differ slightly or significantly with equivalent features in earlier versions because some of the these features work differently in Photoshop 4.0.

Other Resources

The techniques presented in this book do not require any software application (other than Photoshop) to complete. Nor do they require the use of any third-party plug-ins, except for the animation presented in Chapter 12, "Web Graphics: Creating an Animated Gear System," which requires a third-party application to assemble the individual frames into an animation because this cannot be done within Photoshop. Nevertheless, numerous applications can be used to accomplish the task and some suggested resources are provided with the technique.

System Requirements

Photoshop 4.0 is available for both the Macintosh and PC platforms. The techniques of this book can be completed regardless of the specific platform on which you work. It's also important to note that the techniques of this book do not require any capabilities beyond the minimum that Adobe recommends. Actual requirements, however, will vary depending on the sizes of the images that are to be edited within the application. It's also important to note that additional RAM above the recommended minimum will help to improve the performance of the application. The following requirements were derived from Adobe's recommendations:

Macintosh Users:

- Machines with a 68030 processor (or higher) model with System 7.1 and higher, or Power Macintosh machines with System 7.1.2 or higher. System software 7.5 is preferred.

- 16 megabytes (MB) of RAM for application use; 32 MB or more is preferred.

- 25 MB of free disk space for installation. Additional space required when working with large files.

- Color display with 8-bit (256 color) video card; 24-bit (true color) video is preferred.

- CD-ROM drive.

PC Users:

- PC equipped with 386 and higher processors, Windows 3.1 running with MS-DOS 5.0 or higher, Windows 95, or Intel-based Windows NT Desktop 3.5.1 or higher. Pentium II processor or higher preferred.

- 16 MB of RAM for application use. 32 MB or more preferred.

- 25 MB of free disk space for installation. Additional space required when working with large files.

- Color display with 8-bit (256 color) video card. 24-bit (true color) video card preferred.

- CD-ROM drive.

The Techniques

All of the images in this book have been developed in the RGB mode and most of those have been developed at 300 dpi with only a few exceptions. Each technique is presented in a step-by-step manner and each step contains concisely worded instructions accompanied by screen shots of dialog boxes to show the appropriate settings for the operations that are implemented.

The Blue Type

As you work through the steps, you will see phrases that are colored light blue. These same phrases are listed in alphabetical order in the "Photoshop Basics" chapter. If a blue highlighted phrase instructs you to perform a task that you are not familiar with, simply look the phrase up in the Basics chapter where you'll find more detailed instructions for completing the involved operations. Advanced users can perform the task as they normally would.

Menu Commands

You'll also see instructions that look like this:

Filter➡Blur➡Gaussian Blur (Radius: 2 pixels)

In this case, the instruction is telling you to apply the Gaussian Blur filter and provides you with all the information you need to navigate the menus system. To apply the filter, click the Filter menu at the top of the screen and drag down to the Blur option. Once the Blur option is highlighted, a new menu will open to the right so that you can select the Gaussian Blur filter.

A dialog box will now appear so that you can adjust the specific settings with which the filter will be applied. In this case, the value of the sole setting (Radius: 2 pixels) is specified in parentheses behind the instruction and this is how the dialog box settings are given in the text of each technique. In some cases, the settings will be specified outside of parentheses, but the information will always be provided immediately after the instruction. Once you have adjusted the setting, choose OK to apply the filter.

Photoshop Basics

The goal of this section is to help new and novice users of Photoshop with the simple, basic tasks required to create the techniques and sample images of this book. However, it might also be necessary for advanced users to refer to this section on occasion to see which methods are prescribed for completing specific operations.

This chapter assumes that you're working in Photoshop 4.0 and that you're also keeping the toolbox as well as all the palettes open. However, keep in mind that the visibility of all these items can easily be toggled from within the Window menu. Please note that keyboard shortcuts for the Macintosh version of Photoshop appear in parentheses (), while brackets [] are used to contain all Windows-based shortcuts.

The Tools Palette

If you're not familiar with a specific tool in the Photoshop toolbox, there's no reason to panic. In fact, it rarely takes new users of the application long to familiarize themselves with the functions of all the tools that it contains. Nevertheless, the toolbox is provided below with callouts which you may use as a reference to quickly locate tools that are called for in the text of the chapters.

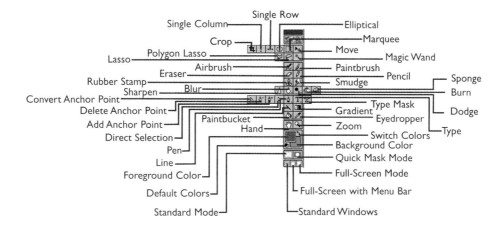

Basic Photoshop Tasks

Each of the basic tasks described below corresponds to the blue highlighted text in the chapters that follow. Here, you can easily find the instructions you need for performing a particular Photoshop task. In fact, all of the tasks are alphabetically listed so that you can quickly locate information as needed.

Adjust the Layer Opacity

To adjust the layer opacity for a particular layer, first click the layer name in the Layers palette to make it active and then adjust the opacity slider at the top of the Layers palette.

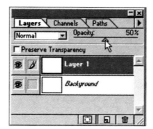

Change the Layer Apply Mode

To change the Layer Apply mode for a particular layer, first click the layer name in the Layers palette to make it active and then select the desired mode from the list of options in the pulldown menu located at the top of the palette.

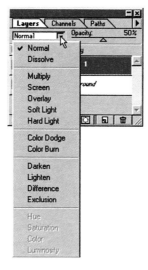

Create Layer Drop Shadows

In this book, the creation of layer drop shadows will be treated as basic operations because they're used so often throughout the text. Whenever you're instructed to create a layer drop shadow, use either one of the two actions provided on the *Photoshop Magic: Expert Edition* CD-ROM. The following details will instruct you on how to load the actions and play them to create layer drop shadows.

Load the Actions from the CD-ROM

To load the actions, choose the Load Actions command from the Actions palette pull-out menu and select the file named SHADOW.ACT located in the Basics folder on the CD-ROM. Two versions of the action will now be appended to the list of actions that the palette may have already contained. The version marked (Default) will play with default settings that work well with the techniques of this book. There may be occasions, however, where you might want to specify your own settings in which case you can play the action marked (Options) instead.

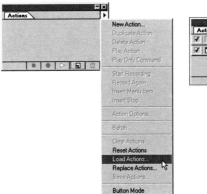

When creating layer drop shadows, keep in mind that the drop shadow will be created for the layer that is active at the time that the action is played.

Play the Action with Default Settings

Shortcut: Press F10.

To play the action with the default settings, click the Drop Shadow (Default) action in the Actions palette to make it active. Now click the Play button at the bottom of the palette. The action will now play without interruption to create a drop shadow below the layer that is currently active.

Play the Action with User-Defined Settings

Shortcut: Press Shift+F10.

To play the action with user-defined settings, click the Drop Shadow (Options) action in the Actions palette to make it active. Now click the Play button at the bottom of the palette.

The action will next display a series of dialog boxes in which you can alter the default settings that are displayed.

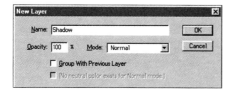
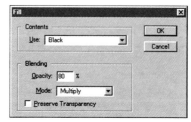
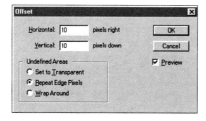

Tip

When playing this action, it's recommended that you use the New Layer dialog box for the sole purpose of naming the new layer to be created. Use the Fill dialog box for the sole purpose of specifying the Opacity (the darkness) of the resulting shadow, and the Offset dialog box to specify pixel offset values that offset the shadow by roughly twice the pixel radius that you specify in the Gaussian Blur dialog box, which appears last. To avoid potential complications in the future, layer merging operations involving the drop shadow that is created, it's also recommended that you leave all other input fields set to their default values as the action plays.

Create a New Channel/Layer/Path

In this case, the operation is the same regardless of which palette you're working in. To create a new channel/layer/path, simply click the Create New Channel/Layer/Path icon at the bottom of the palette or choose the New Channel/Layer/Path command from the palette pullout menu.

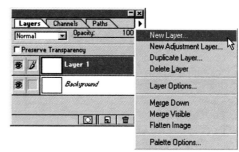

The new layer will now appear in the palette as the active layer above the layer that was previously active.

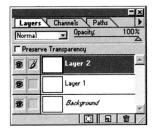

Tip

Holding the (Option)[Alt] key while clicking the New Channel/Layer/Path icon causes the New Channel/Layer/Path dialog box to be displayed so that you may specify a name instead of accepting the default. In fact, this feature should be used whenever you're instructed to create a new channel/layer/path followed by a name in quotation marks (in other words, Create a new layer named Layer Name). Keep in mind that default names are always given in parentheses.

Create a New File

Shortcuts: Press (Command+N)[Ctrl+N].

To create a new file, choose File➡New.

The New dialog box will now appear so that you can name your new file and establish other settings as well.

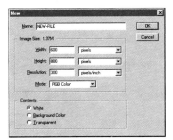

Delete a Channel/Layer/Path

In this case, the operation is the same regardless of which palette you're working in. To delete a channel/layer/path, place the cursor over the channel/layer/path that you wish to delete and drag it down over the Trash icon at the bottom of the palette (just like you would to get rid of a document on the desktop). If the channel/layer/path that you want to delete is active, you may also simply click the Trash icon without dragging the channel/layer/path to it, or you can choose the Delete Channel/Layer/Path command from the palette pullout menu.

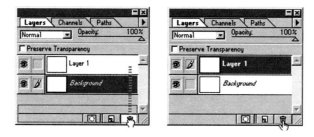

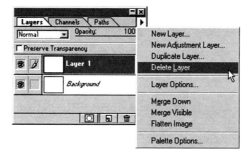

Deselect a Selection

Shortcuts: Press (Command+D)[Control+D].

To deselect a selection, choose Select➟None and the marquee will then disappear.

Duplicate a Channel/Layer/Path

The operation is the same regardless of which palette you're working in. To create a duplicate of a channel/layer/path, place the cursor over the channel/layer/path that you wish to duplicate and then drag it down over the Create New Channel/Layer/Path icon at the bottom of the palette. If the channel/layer/path that you wish to duplicate is already active, you may also choose the Duplicate Channel/Layer/Path command from the palette pullout menu.

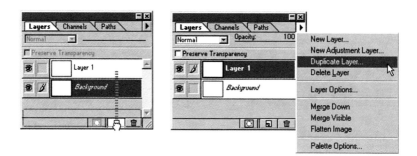

A new copy of the channel/layer/path that you duplicated will now appear in the palette as well.

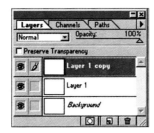

Enter the Text

Two Type tools are in Photoshop 4.0: the standard Type tool and the Type Mask tool. Each effect in this book specifies which Type tool to use.

Before entering the text using the standard Type tool, make sure that the foreground color is set to your desired text color. When adding text to an image, the standard Type tool will create a new layer for the type whereas the Type Mask tool will create a selection border in the shape of the text instead. Fill the selection with the desired color.

To enter the text, select the Type tool that you want to use and then click anywhere in the image to open the Type Tool dialog box. Type the text in the large box at the bottom of the dialog box and then make your attribute choices from the options in the upper section of the dialog box. Unless noted otherwise, always turn on the Anti-Aliased and Left Justification options as shown for the effects in this book.

After clicking OK, move the type into position with the Move (standard Type tool) or Marquee (Type Mask tool) tool.

Enter/Exit Quick Mask Mode

Shortcut: Press Q to enter and exit the Quick Mask mode.

Click the Quick Mask icon in the Tools palette to switch to Quick Mask mode; conversely, click the Standard mode icon to return to Standard mode.

Essentially a Quick Mask is a temporary channel. When you're in Quick Mask mode you can use any of the Photoshop tools and functions to change the selection without changing the image. When you switch back to Standard mode you'll have a new selection.

Quick Mask mode

Standard mode

Fill a Channel/Layer/Selection

In this case, the text assumes that you're performing all fill operations in the same way. To fill a channel/layer/selection, simply choose Edit➡Fill.

This causes the Fill dialog box to appear. Unless otherwise instructed, all fills should be performed at an opacity of 100% in the Normal mode.

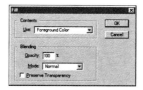

Tip

When working with layers, keep in mind that the Preserve Transparency option must be turned off whenever you wish to fill a transparent region. This doesn't mean, however, that you should routinely turn off this option whenever you perform a fill operation because there are times when the text will require you to perform a fill with the Preserve Transparency option turned on. This option is located in the top left of the Layers palette.

Invert the Selection

Shortcuts: Press (Command+Shift+I)[Control+Shift+I] to select everything except what is currently selected.

To invert a selection, choose Select➡Inverse.

Link/Unlink Layers and Layer Masks

To link/unlink a layer with the active layer, simply click in the second column of the layer that you want to link. This toggles the Link icon on or off.

To link/unlink a layer mask, simply click between the image and the mask thumbnails that appear on the layer. The layer need not be active.

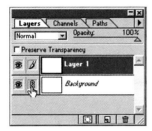 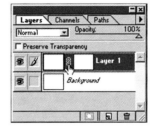

Load a Layer Transparency Selection

Shortcut: Hold the (Command)[Control] key and click the layer (in the Layers palette) from which you want the selection to be loaded.

To load a layer transparency selection, make the layer from which you wish to load the selection active and then choose Select➡Load. In the Load Selection dialog box that now appears, select the Layer Transparency option in the Channel field and then specify the remaining parameters as required.

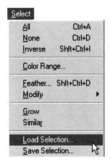 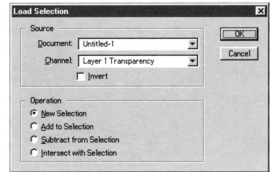

Load a Selection

Shortcut: Hold the (Command)[Control] key and click on the channel (in the Channels palette) that contains the selection you want to load.

To load a selection, choose Select➡Load Selection. This brings up the Load Selection dialog box where you can specify the name of the channel that you wish to load as well as other parameters.

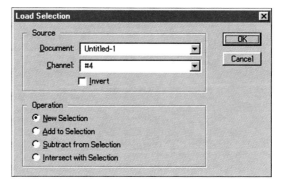

Make a Channel/Layer/Path Active

This operation is the same regardless of the palette in which you're working. To make a channel/layer/path active for editing or modification, click its thumbnail or title in the Channels/Layers/Paths palette. Once the layer is active, it will become highlighted.

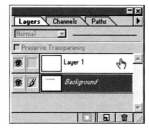
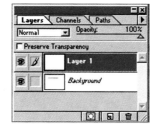

You can tell the channel is active, if it is highlighted with a color.

Make a Channel/Layer Visible/Invisible

This operation is the same for channels and layers. To make a channel/layer visible, click the left-most column of the channel/layers that you wish to make visible. If the Eye icon appears, then the channel/layer is visible. If the column is empty, then that channel/layer is made invisible.

Merge Layers

Shortcuts: Press (Command+E)[Ctrl+E].

To merge down a layer with an underlying layer, simply choose Layer➡Merge Down. Keep in mind that both layers must be visible in order to be merged. To merge a linked list of layers, simply choose Layer➡Merge Linked. In this case, linked layers that are not visible will be discarded without warning.

Open a File

To open a file, choose File➡Open File. In the dialog box that appears, specify the filename and location of the file that you wish to open.

Place a Horizontal/Vertical Guide

Shortcuts: Press (Command+;)[Ctrl+;] to show guides and press (Command+R)[Ctrl+R] to show rulers.

To add a vertical or horizontal guide, choose View➡Show Guides and View➡Show Rulers (if these features are not already visible).

With any tool selected, drag a guide from either the horizontal or vertical ruler. To align the guide with a ruler position, hold down the Shift key as you drag the guide. To adjust the position of a previously placed guide, select the Move tool first.

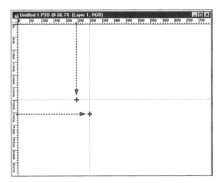

Tip

As you drag the guide, hold down the (Option)[Alt] key to switch between horizontal or vertical guides, or vice versa.

Renaming a Channel/Layer/Path

The operation is the same regardless of the palette in which you're working. To rename a channel/layer/path, make it active and then double-click the channel/layer/path that you wish to rename.

In the dialog box that now appears, enter a new name. In the Channels/Layers palette, the dialog box that appears is the Channel/Layer Options dialog box. In the Paths palette, the dialog box is the Rename Dialog Box. Nevertheless, each of the dialog boxes provides a name field where a new name can be specified.

Reset a Tool

Once a tool has been selected from the toolbox, you have the option of resetting the parameters of the tool to the Photoshop defaults regardless of the tool that is selected. To reset a tool, choose the Reset Tool command from the tool's Options palette pullout menu. In some cases, Photoshop will then prompt you with an inquiry dialog box. When this occurs, the text will instruct you on how to proceed.

Save a File

Shortcuts: Press (Command+S)[Ctrl+S].

To save a file, choose File➡Save As. This displays the Save As dialog box, where you name your new file and choose a format in which to save it.

File format selection depends on what you have in your file, what you want to keep when you save it, and what you're going to do with the file after it is saved. Consult a detailed Photoshop book, such as *Photoshop 4 Complete* or *Adobe Photoshop Classroom in a Book*, for more guidance on which file format is best for your needs.

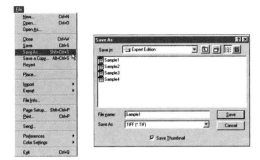

Save a Selection

Shortcut: Click the New Channel icon at the bottom of the Channels palette.

To save a selection, choose Select➥Save Selection. In the Save Selection dialog box that now appears, select the New option in the Channel field.

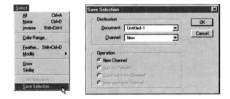

The Channels palette will now display the new channel.

Tip

Holding the (Option)[Alt] key while clicking the Save Selection icon at the bottom of the Channels palette causes the Channel Options dialog box to be displayed so that you can specify a name instead of accepting the default. In fact, this feature should be used whenever you're instructed to save a selection to a new channel followed by a name in quotation marks (in other words, Save the selection to a new channel named Channel Name). Keep in mind that default names are always given parentheses.

Set the Foreground/Background Colors

To change the Foreground or Background color, click either the Foreground icon or the Background icon.

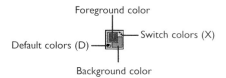

Foreground color

Switch colors (X)

Default colors (D)

Background color

The Color Picker dialog box appears, which enables you to choose a new foreground or background color by moving and clicking the cursor (now a circle) along the spectrum box, or by changing specific RGB, CMYK, or other percentage values.

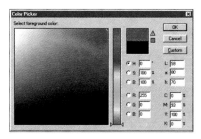

Note that the Foreground and Background icons on the Tools palette now reflect your color choices.

Switch to the Default Colors

Shortcut: Press D to switch to the default foreground and background colors.

To change the foreground and background colors to black and white respectively, click on the Default Colors icon.

Default colors

Switch the Foreground and Background Colors

Shortcut: Press X to switch the foreground and background colors.

To switch the foreground and background colors, click on the Switch Colors icon located in the toolbox. This flips the two colors shown in this icon only and does not affect the rest of the image.

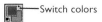

Switch colors

Simulating Stained Glass

Stained glass is often described as the art of manipulating colored light, but stained glass is much more than just an art form. It's also a craft that has experienced continuous evolution from the Middle Ages to the present day.

Nevertheless, the raw materials of the medium have remained much the same. They basically include lead and glass. Light is often considered to be a raw material of the medium as well, but it's not a variable over which the artist has direct control. Instead, it's an indirect variable that the artist controls by varying the color and texture of the glass as well as the placement of the lead. The lead is often thought of as just the glue that holds the individual pieces of glass together, but it's role is more significant than that. In fact, the lead is often used to define a design more clearly by blocking light along lines that form a stencil.

When simulating stained glass designs in Photoshop, it's important to consider the characteristics of the individual materials and how they are used. It's also important to consider the approach that is often followed when implementing a design in the art form as well. As already mentioned, stained glass designs are often implemented from stencils, and we'll begin developing the sample image of this technique in the same way. We'll then use the stencil as the framework for the individual operations that must be performed to introduce color and texture for simulating the glass. The real stars of this technique, however, are the layer apply modes and the color editing controls that we'll use to edit the glass textures so that they appear to be transmitting light instead of reflecting it.

Creating the Stencil

In this case, we'll be creating the stencil using the paths capability to trace out contours in an existing image. The image that we'll be using was scanned in from a pencil sketch with lines that are not uniform in thickness. The image also exhibits smudge marks, but these characteristics don't pose any problems and instead of cleaning up the image directly, we'll use the paths capability to trace out the lines of the stencil so that we can reconstruct a clean version of it.

By using Photoshop's vector-based paths capability, we also gain a degree of flexibility that we wouldn't otherwise have because we can now redraw a high quality version of the stencil at any resolution, at any time, and with any pixel width that we desire. In fact, we'll take advantage of this capability to redraw the stencil more than once which ultimately will lead to a higher-quality final image. We'll begin by tracing out the paths.

1 Open the file named Coyote.PSD. In the Paths palette, notice that a path named Default has already been defined. This is the path that was used to produce the sample images that accompany this technique. If you want to define your own path, create a new path named Stencil. Now use the Pen tool as well as the other path editing tools found in the same flyout menu of the toolbox to define subpaths that trace out the hand-sketched stencil of the image. Once you've completed the Stencil path, make sure that it remains active before moving on to the next step. If you do not want to define your own path, make the Default path active at this time.

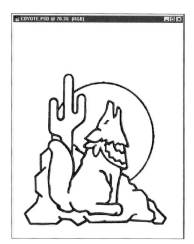

2 Select the Paintbrush tool from the Toolbox. In the Brushes palette, choose the New Brush command from the palette pull-out menu. In the New Brush dialog box that now appears, adjust the settings to (Diameter: 8 pixels, Hardness: 100%, Spacing: 25%). The new brush will now be selected in the Brushes palette.

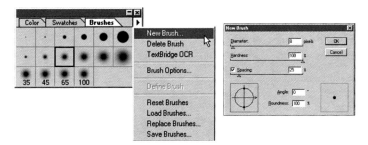

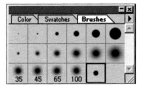

The borders of the stencil have now been redrawn on the clean, white backdrop of the Background layer. The stroked lines were produced with black using the Paintbrush tool and the medium, hard brush defined in the previous step. In this case, the narrow width of the stencil borders was chosen to define separate regions into which we'll now introduce color. Another stencil will be drawn with wider borders that we'll use to create the lead between the individual regions of simulated glass.

3 Switch to the default colors. With the Background layer still active, fill the layer with the background color. In the Paths palette, choose the Stroke Path command from the palette pull-out menu and then choose the Turn Off Path command from the same menu as well.

Simulating Colored Glass

We're now ready to begin producing the stained glass effect. As we proceed, we'll make use of multiple filters to produce more than one glass texture in the image, but there is one filter that we'll consistently rely upon. This filter is the Plastic Wrap filter, which produces a smooth, glasslike appearance when it is applied. It also produces a lot of white highlights.

In nature, white highlights are typically associated with regions of over-saturation that are produced when strong light is reflected off a smooth surface, but our goal is to produce a textured surface that appears to be transmitting light instead. In fact, one of the main differences between transmitted and reflected light is that transmitted light tends to produce regions that are fully saturated without being over-saturated. Therefore, we'll have to modify the resulting texture of the Plastic Wrap filter to eliminate the white highlights that it produces. This is actually quite easy to implement, and we'll accomplish the task with the use of the layer apply modes and the color editing features that Photoshop provides. As you'll soon see, the resulting effect is quite realistic. Let's begin by introducing a stained glass texture to the coyote.

1 Create a new layer named Coyote. Select the Magic Wand tool from the toolbox. In the Magic Wand Options palette, reset the tool and then turn on the Sample Merged option. Now use the Magic Wand tool to select the head and the body of the coyote. Set the foreground color to orange (R: 255 G: 180 B: 0) and then fill the selection with the foreground color. Now deselect the selection.

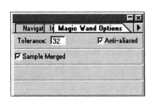

In this case, the Add Noise and Gaussian Blur filters were used to provide a subtle texture, which was then used by the Plastic Wrap filter to produce the resulting, glass-like texture. The texture, however, now exhibits the unwanted regions of over-saturation that were previously mentioned, and they now need to be removed.

2 Choose Filter➡Noise➡Add Noise (Amount: 30, Distribution: Uniform, Monochromatic: Checked) and then choose Filter➡Blur➡Gaussian Blur (Radius: 1.0 pixels). Now choose Filter➡Artistic➡Plastic Wrap (Highlight Strength: 15, Detail: 15, Smoothness: 4).

3 Choose Image➡Adjust➡Hue/Saturation (Hue: 0, Saturation: 100, Lightness: -30). With the Coyote layer still active, duplicate the layer and then change the layer apply mode of the duplicate layer (Coyote copy) to Multiply. Make the Coyote layer active. Now link the duplicate layer to the active layer and then merge the linked layers. The over-saturation has now been removed and the appearance of the simulated glass looks much more natural. Let's now move on to add a glass texture to the perimeter region.

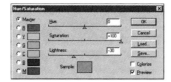

Simulating White, Frosted Glass

Before we proceed, it's important to note that we'll be creating a glass-like texture with a similar appearance to the one that we just created in the previous section. But the resulting texture will differ from the previous texture in that it will not exhibit any color—it will essentially be a grayscale texture. As a result, we won't be able to adjust the appearance of the texture with the controls of the Hue/Saturation dialog box. Instead, we'll use the controls of the Brightness/Contrast dialog box.

In this case, it's also important to note that the appearance of white pixels in the texture is perfectly acceptable since the fully saturated state of a white region is white. Therefore, we'll be more concerned with the task of controlling the overall balance of white pixels to non-white pixels instead of eliminating them completely. In fact, this balance can be controlled to a large extent in the Plastic Wrap dialog box with the Detail slider control. Let's now move on to create the texture.

I Create a new layer named Perimeter. Now use the Magic Wand tool to select the perimeter region of the image. Switch to the default colors and then switch the foreground and background colors. Now fill the selection with the foreground color and then deselect the selection.

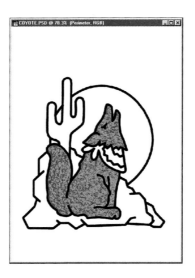

2 Choose Filter➥Noise➥Add Noise (Amount: 30, Distribution: Uniform, Monochromatic: Checked). If necessary, use the hand tool to move a non-transparent portion of the Perimeter layer into view if you want to preview the filter before accepting the settings that you define.

Now choose Filter➥Blur➥Gaussian Blur (Radius: 1.0 pixels) and then choose Filter➥Artistic➥Plastic Wrap. In the dialog box that appears, adjust the Highlight slider to 15 and the Smoothness slider to 4. Now adjust the Detail slider through its entire range. Notice how this affects the balance of fully saturated pixels in the resulting texture. When you are done, set the Detail slider to 13 before accepting the settings. This produces a texture that already looks quite good, but let's make some small adjustment to enhance the existing detail. Choose Image➥Adjust➥Brightness/Contrast (Brightness: -20, Contrast: +20).

As you can see, the resulting texture looks very realistic. In fact, we've even taken advantage of an artifact of the Plastic Wrap filter that I suspect would not be desired in most other situations. Notice that the resulting texture is not uniform across the entire perimeter region. In fact, the pixels in the corners are more fully saturated than the pixels closer to the center. This is an artifact of the

continues

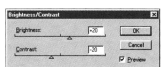

continued

Plastic Wrap filter that becomes more pronounced as you lower the Detail slider control. In this case, I think the effect adds some realism to the final image. Therefore, I chose a value of 13 for the Detail slider setting instead of the value of 15 that was used when producing the texture for the Coyote. Now let's move on to introduce some additional textures with differing appearances to increase visual interest.

Incorporating Different Textures

1 Create a new layer named Terrain. Now hold the Shift key and use the Magic Wand tool to select the three regions that form the terrain upon which the coyote sits. In order to create this next texture, we're going to make use of the Motion Blur filter, which often produces unwanted edge effects. Therefore, we'll oversize the current selection to complete the texture. Then we'll clip the texture so that it fits properly into the regions defined by the stencil. Choose Select➡Modify➡Expand (16 pixels). Now set the foreground color to magenta (R: 255 G: 0 B: 230) and then fill the selection with the foreground color. Deselect the selection.

Up until now, we've only introduced one texture into the image with the two types of glass that we've already simulated. Nevertheless, it's important to add a variety of textures to increase visual interest, and there are many ways in which this can be done. In fact, this section will instruct you on how to create two more sample textures, and I'm sure you'll agree that the additional textures really make a big difference in the final image.

2 Choose Filter➡Noise➡Add Noise (Amount: 70, Distribution: Uniform, Monochromatic: Checked) and then choose Filter➡Blur➡Motion Blur (Angle: 45 degrees, Distance: 30 pixels). Now choose Filter➡Artistic➡Plastic Wrap (Highlight Strength: 15, Detail: 15, Smoothness: 4). In the next step, we'll edit the color of the texture before clipping it to properly fit into the regions defined by the stencil.

3 Choose Image➥Adjust➥Hue/Saturation (Hue: 0, Saturation: 100, Lightness: -30). With the Terrain layer still active, duplicate the layer and then change the Layer Apply mode of the duplicate (Terrain copy) to Multiply. Now make the Terrain layer active. Link the duplicate layer to the active layer and then merge the linked layers.

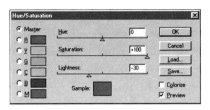

4 This texture looks great, but it still needs to be trimmed to properly fit into the borders defined by the stencil. Make the Terrain layer invisible. Now hold the Shift key and use the Magic Wand tool to reselect the three regions of the terrain. Invert the selection and then make the Terrain layer visible once again. Now press Delete to trim the texture on the Terrain layer and deselect the selection. We'll now move on to create one additional texture.

5 Create a new layer named Moon. Now use the Magic Wand tool to select the three regions that form the moon. Set the foreground color to yellow (R: 255 G: 255 B: 0) and then fill the selection with the foreground color. Deselect the selection.

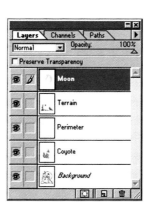

6 Choose Filter➡Texture➡Texturizer (Texture: Canvas, Scaling: 200%, Relief: 4, Light Direction: Top Right). Now choose Filter➡Blur➡Gaussian Blur (Radius: 1.5 pixels) and then choose Filter➡Artistic➡Plastic Wrap (Highlight Strength: 10, Detail: 14, Smoothness: 5).

7 Choose Image➡Adjust➡Hue/Saturation (Hue: 0, Saturation: 100, Lightness: -30). Duplicate the layer and then change the layer apply mode of the duplicate (Moon copy) to Multiply. Now make the Moon layer active. Link the duplicate layer to the active layer and then merge the linked layers.

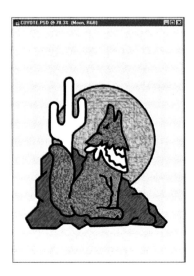

8 At this point, the technique has presented all the textures that I used to complete the sample image. Feel free to use any of these textures or define your own to complete the remaining regions of the image. For the cactus I used the texture presented in steps 1 through 4 of this section, and for the bandanna I used the texture presented in the section titled "Simulating Colored Glass." Once you've completed the remaining regions, choose Layer➡Flatten Image.

Simulating the Leading

Now that we've filled all the regions with simulated glass, we can go ahead and simulate the leading. It's important to note that the leading was saved for last so that we could use it to cover up the rough edges of the glass. As you'll soon see, the leading cleans things up quite nicely and really enhances the image.

1 Select the Paintbrush tool from the toolbox. In the Brushes palette, select the brush that you defined in step 2 of the section titled "Creating the Stencil." Now select the Brush Options command from the palette pullout menu. In the Brush Options dialog box that now appears, set the Diameter to 10 and the Hardness to 0%.

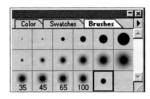
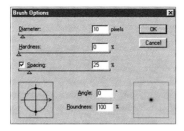

2 Create a new channel (Channel #4) and then switch to the default colors. In the Paths palette, make the Stencil path active and then choose the Stroke Path command from the palette pull-out menu.

3 In the Brushes palette, select the Brush Options command from the palette pullout menu once again. In the Brush Options dialog box that now appears, leave the Diameter set to 10, but change the Hardness to 85%. Create a new layer named Glass Leading and then set the foreground color to dark gray (R: 60 G: 60 B: 60). With the Stencil path still active, choose the Stroke Path command from the palette pullout menu once more. Now choose Filter➡Render➡Lighting Effects and adjust the settings as shown. Most importantly, make sure to select Channel #4 as the Texture Channel and specify a Height of 6. In the Brushes palette, select the Brush Options command from the palette pullout menu one last time. In the dialog box that now appears, set the Diameter to 5 and the Hardness to 95%. Choose the Stroke Path command from the palette pullout menu and then choose the Turn Off Path command from the pullout menu as well. Now create a layer drop shadow.

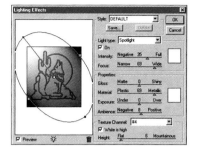

Chapter 2

Simulating Water Reflection

Photoshop Filters are a lot of fun to play around with and can provide a great deal of power for producing a number of special effects. In many cases, it is possible to get away with the use of just one filter to produce the desired outcome in a given project. Take, for example, the Distort filters. With the application of just one of these filters, it's often possible to simulate very realistic water effects, such as reflection off from the rippled surface of a swimming pool.

But what about reflections off from larger bodies of water, such as the reflection of a city skyline off from an adjacent lake or river? This is one of many effects that require a more comprehensive approach using multiple filters to produce the final effect. In developing this technique, it's helpful to study a number of actual photos in order to identify common characteristics that can be simulated with specific filters and other Photoshop controls. These characteristics include the horizontal structure of the waves, the relative intensity of the reflected image, and the vertical blurring that is produced in these types of reflections by variations on the water surface.

Preparing the Reflected Image

In order to create the water reflection effect, we'll have to make room below the current image by increasing the size of the image canvas. In fact, the operations of this section will also show you how to reflect the existing image down and perform some initial operations to begin simulating some of the characteristics that we would expect a large body of water to exhibit. More specifically, we'll simulate vertical streaking of the reflected image, which is a characteristic that large bodies introduce into reflected landscapes whenever the surface of the water is active.

1 Open the file named **FIRE.TIF.** Switch to the default colors and then switch the foreground and background colors.

2 Choose Image➥Canvas Size. In the Canvas Size dialog box, specify a new canvas size of 800 × 1200 pixels and select the top center square as the anchor.

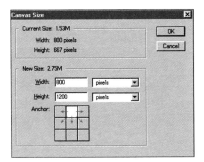

The canvas now provides the additional space required to produce the water reflection effect below the original image. The new area of the canvas that is not covered by the original image has been filled with the background color selected in Step 1 (black).

continues

continued

Because the original height of the image was 667 pixels, it would have been acceptable to increase the canvas size by the same amount in order to provide a reflection of the entire fireworks display. This would have resulted in a final canvas size of 1334 (2 x 667) pixels, but I chose a final height that is less than the maximum allowed so that the reflected image will be cropped, which will help to prevent the reflection from dominating the image. In this case, it's appropriate for the fireworks display to remain the center of focus. Even though the reflection effect is awesome, remember that its purpose is to enhance the existing composition.

3 Select the Magic Wand tool from the toolbox. In the Magic Wand Options palette, reset the tool. Now use the Magic Wand tool to select the newly created region of solid black in the lower portion of the canvas. Invert the selection to select the original image and copy the contents of the selection to the clipboard.

4 Invert the selection once more to reselect the lower portion of the canvas. Choose Edit➨Paste Into to place the contents of the clipboard into the selection area. Photoshop will deactivate the selection automatically.

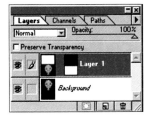

5 Choose Layer➨Transform➨Flip Vertical to flip the image on Layer 1. Now use the Move tool to align the image on Layer 1 below the original image.

It is important to understand how the Paste Into command differs from the more commonly used Paste command. Notice that the previous operation results not only in the creation of a new layer (Layer 1) but also a layer mask. In the Layers palette, a thumbnail image of the Layer mask now appears on Layer 1. This mask has also been saved to a channel because this is how Photoshop saves all masks and selections.

In the Channels palette, make note of the Layer 1 Mask channel that resides directly below the RGB color channels in the Channels palette. This channel and the mask that appears in the Layers palette are one and the same. Therefore, any changes made to the Layer 1 Mask channel automatically effect how the content of Layer 1 is displayed. Keep in mind that Layer 1 still contains the entire image although the layer mask is limiting the display of that image to the region that was originally defined by the selection that we pasted into.

These filters were applied to add abstraction to the reflected image and create vertical streaking, which is almost always present in large body water reflections. The amount of vertical streaking is determined by the roughness of the water that you want to simulate. Use lower values to simulate calm water and larger values to simulate rough water. Keep in mind that even calm water produces quite a bit of vertical streaking so you will not need to vary the setting by much.

6 Choose Filter➡Noise➡Add Noise (Amount: 20, Distribution: Gaussian, Monochromatic: Checked). Since the Noise filter is applied only to the non-transparent regions of Layer 1, you most likely will not see anything in the preview window. Place the cursor over the preview window so that the hand tool appears, and then drag a non-transparent region of Layer 1 into view so that you can preview the effect before the filter is applied. Now choose Filter➡Blur➡Gaussian Blur (Radius: 5) and then choose Filter➡Blur➡Motion Blur (Angle: 90 degrees, Distance: 200 pixels).

Simulating the Structure of Waves

Even though we've already introduced vertical streaking, we still need to simulate the structure of waves in order to create a realistic effect, and we'll do this by preparing a mask that we'll then apply to the image in the last step of this section.

1 Duplicate the Layer 1 Mask channel and then rename the channel to Waves. Photoshop will automatically make the Waves channel active and visible. Photoshop will also turn off the visibility of all other channels so that the image window now displays only the mask. The upper portion of the image window is now solid black and the lower portion is solid white. In the next several steps, this mask will be edited to produce a distinct wave pattern and will then be applied to the image.

2 Load the selection from the Waves channel. This creates a rectangular selection border around the white region of the mask so that editing operations are restricted to the region where the water reflection effect is to be generated. Choose Filter➡Noise➡Add Noise (Amount: 999, Distribution: Gaussian, Monochromatic: Checked).

The amount of 999 is used to create high contrast, which is needed to produce waves that are distinct in appearance. In our case, this is important since the wave pattern must be distinguishable in the image, which is already quite dark and will remain so. High contrast also produces waves that have more detail that is not desired in this particular image because we would not expect to see a lot of detail in a wave pattern at night. There are several ways, however, that unwanted detail can be easily removed in later steps. Therefore, it is best to maintain high contrast in the mask until the wave structure has been produced. Then you can remove unwanted detail just before applying the mask to the image.

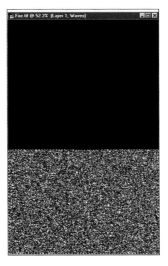

3 Choose Filter➡Blur➡Motion Blur (Angle: 0 degrees, Distance: 20).

At this point, the final effect is not particularly sensitive to the distance setting of the Motion Blur filter. The distance value, however, must be high enough to produce a definite wave pattern. High distance values can also cause undesirable edge distortions that you will most likely want to avoid. The angle setting determines the direction of the wave pattern and it may be varied to simulate waves moving in different directions.

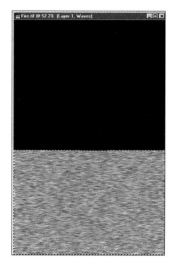

4 Notice that the contrast of the mask was decreased by the operation in the previous step. Choose Image➡Adjust➡Threshhold (Level: 160).

As you can see, this increases the contrast of the image quite dramatically. The individual waves are now quite distinct, which will be necessary in order to make the wave pattern stand out in the final image. In this case, a number of different controls can be used to increase the contrast of the mask.

For example, we could have used the controls in either the Brightness/Contrast or the Levels dialog boxes. These would have produced similar effects. I decided to use the Threshold command because it is better at reducing some of the unwanted detail mentioned earlier. Notice the rugged appearance that the mask now exhibits. If used without any

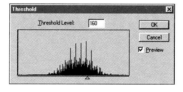

5 Choose Filter➡Blur➡Motion Blur (Angle: 0 degrees, Distance 35 pixels). In this case, the angle should always be chosen to match the direction of the existing wave pattern. Also, the Gaussian Blur filter could have been used instead to produce an acceptable variation.

continues

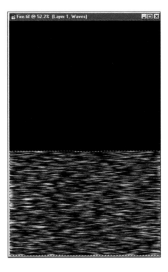

continued

modification, the mask will tend to produce the appearance of waves that are more active. In this case, I wanted to produce a more calm appearance in the waves of the final image. Therefore, we will soften the mask before proceeding on.

Actually, I recommend that the mask be softened by at least a small amount, even if the desired final effect is to produce waves that are more rough in appearance. In its present condition, the mask is probably a bit too rugged to produce a realistic effect.

6 Select the Gradient tool from the toolbox. In the Gradient Tool Options palette, reset the tool and then choose Cancel when prompted. Now select the Foreground to Transparent option in the Gradient field. Drag out a gradient from pixel location (400,670) to (400,1100). That's it! The mask is now complete and ready to use.

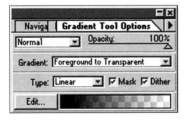

At this point, the mask is looking quite good and could produce a very realistic effect without further modification, but there's one characteristic of the mask that isn't quite right. In the real world, distant objects appear to have less detail than objects nearby. Therefore, we would expect the distant waves along the horizon of our image to have less noticeable detail than the waves in the foreground. This is one of many potential cues that the human brain uses to interpret the relative positions of objects in a scene and is often overlooked by less experienced Photoshop artists. Nevertheless, this concept can be accommodated by attenuating the mask with the Gradient tool before moving on.

7 Load the selection from the Waves channel. If you have used the exact settings provided in all the previous steps, the current selection will look quite unremarkable. Photoshop draws the selection border by applying a 50% threshold to the grayscale values of the mask in the Waves channel. In this case, only a few of the image pixels will actually appear to be selected, but do not be alarmed. Because this selection was created from a mask, Photoshop will use the greyscale values in the mask instead of the selection borders to determine how individual pixels of the image will be affected when editing operations are performed.

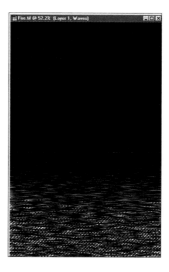

8 Make the RGB channel active. Photoshop will automatically make the RGB channel visible and turn off the visibility of the Waves channel. At this point, Layer 1 should still be the active layer.

9 Now press Delete to begin filling the selection area with the background color. Press Delete again to continue to darken in the structure of the waves if desired. I produced the accompanying image by pressing Delete three times. Now deselect the selection and adjust the layer opacity to 65% to reduce the intensity of the reflected image.

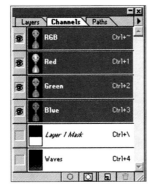

When working with other images, it is likely that you'll need to experiment by using different settings in the steps previously executed. Unfortunately, this technique relies on several steps to prepare the mask before it is applied to the image, so you won't be able to immediately see the effect that varying a particular setting will have. Instead, you'll have to wait until Step 15 when the mask is finally applied.

At this point, you may find that the resulting pattern is not quite what you expected, but instead of immediately starting over, try making some modifications by applying some of the same filters that were used earlier to create the mask in the first place. For example, if you chose different settings with the intent of producing a rugged appearance and now find that the result is too

Painting the Landscape

At this point, the reflection looks very realistic, but the overall image is a different story. In fact, the image is lacking detail along the horizon that is needed by the viewer to properly place the fireworks display and the reflection into a meaningful context. Although the wave structure already provides us with a depth cue, you'll soon see that the addition of landscape along the horizon is the key element that begins to pull all of the image elements together. In this case, we'll use the painting tools to create the landscape from scratch.

continues

continued

rugged, try reapplying the Motion Blur filter to soften the effect. In this example, I did not modify the resulting image in any way.

1 Switch to the default colors. In the Brushes palette, select a brush with a large soft tip.

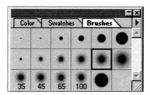

Now create a new layer (Layer 2). Now use the Paintbrush tool to paint in a distant landscape along the horizon. Switch to smaller brushes to add finer detail if desired.

When working with other images, selections may result in colors that are much more vivid, which is undesirable. Pastel shades work best because they tend to be bright and dull in appearance. If the most prominent color is not a pastel, select it anyway. Then click the foreground color in the toolbox to access the Color Picker dialog box and select an off-white shade of the same color. It is also acceptable to use white in most cases for a final effect that is only slightly less realistic if at all.

2 Now use the Eyedropper tool to set the foreground color to an appropriate color that can be used to create distant highlights along the top edge of the landscape that we just painted, as well as on the surface of the water just below the horizon. When selecting a color, choose the most prominent color in the fireworks display. In this case, there are two prominent colors to choose from and it's best to use the color that is closest to white. My selection resulted in a foreground color of pale yellow (R:238 G:221 B:205).

3 Load the transparency selection from Layer 2 and then create a new layer (Layer 3). This layer and the current selection will be used to place the distant highlights along the top edge of the .

landscape that we painted in the first step of this section. Choose Edit➡Stroke (Width: 1 pixel, Location: Inside, Opacity: 100%).

Notice that the landscape was stroked on all sides, which is not desirable. Use the Eraser tool to erase all stroking that does not reside along the top edge of the landscape. Also, erase any areas along the top edge that you would not expect to have direct exposure to the light radiating from the fireworks display.

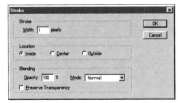

4 Choose Filter➡Blur➡Gaussian Blur (Radius: 3.0 pixels) and then adjust the layer opacity to approximately 30%. These two operations soften the highlights so that they look more natural. Once you're satisfied with the result, merge down Layer 3 with Layer 2.

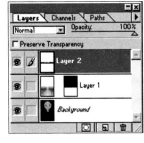

5 Create a new layer (Layer 3). This layer will be used to create highlights on the surface of the water near the horizon. In the

Layers palette, move Layer 3 so that it is placed directly above Layer 1 but below Layer 2. Before proceeding, make sure that Layer 3 is still active.

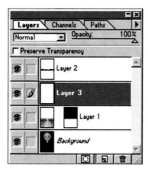

Select the Line tool from the toolbox. In the Line Tool Options palette, reset the tool and then specify a line width of 5 pixels. Now draw a line across the horizon just below the landscape. I started the line from pixel location (0,670).

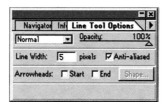

6 Choose Filter➡Blur➡Gaussian Blur (Radius: 30 pixels). This creates a very realistic highlight on the water in the distance—a nice touch! The brightness of this highlight can be adjusted by either changing the opacity of the layer or applying the Gaussian Blur filter with a higher setting. Use the opacity setting when you only want to adjust the intensity of the highlight. Use the Blur filter when you also want to spread the highlight out over a larger area. In this case, I did not reapply the Gaussian Blur filter, but I did adjust the layer opacity to 65%. The image is now complete. If you wish, choose Layer➡Flatten Image and then save the file.

Baking Soda

Chapter 3

Weaving Elements in an Image

Drop shadows are one of the most commonly used tricks for simulating depth when working in Photoshop. With the help of layers, it is easy to control the use of drop shadows to create images that simulate depth by allowing the elements of a layer to cast shadows over the content of underlying layers.

Sometimes, however, it's desirable to create image elements with drop shadows that appear to weave above and below other elements in an image. Unfortunately, this effect is a much more complicated task and requires many steps to complete. In fact, this effect can easily become incredibly difficult to manage when more than just a few image elements are involved. It can also be complicated by image elements with regions that are at least partially transparent.

Fortunately, Photoshop provides a number of advanced capabilities that make it easier to complete complex operations by allowing you to work interchangeably with selections, channels, and masks. Photoshop also provides a number of hot key controls that enable you to combine these items quickly to create composite selections based on boolean logic.

In this technique, we'll produce a generic product label for baking soda, which will include a semi-transparent, yellow ribbon that we'll be weaving through the other elements in the image. By completing this task, the technique will demonstrate how Photoshop's advanced capabilities can be incorporated into an organized approach so we can more easily manage the numerous operations that must be performed to produce the desired effect.

In this example, we'll be following an approach that can easily be generalized to other images containing more elements to be weaved. More specifically, we'll first create the individual elements of the image. Then we'll create selections based on the geometries of those elements that we'll later combine into composite selections. This will enable us to quickly isolate specific regions so that the weaving effect can be produced easily.

In this case, the number of image elements will be kept to a minimum so that the approach is conveyed without complicating the technique with excessive detail. Also, the image elements will be restricted to have fairly simple geometries although advanced operations will be used to produce them. Nevertheless, I'm sure you'll see how the individual operations as well as the overall approach can be generalized to manage tasks that are even more involved than the one at hand.

As you proceed through the individual steps, this technique will also describe some of the basic features of the Info palette that you'll find to be an invaluable tool for completing individual operations more precisely.

Creating the Basic Elements and Selections

The sample image of this chapter will be created from scratch. Therefore, we'll need to create the basic elements of the image before we can implement the operations required to complete the weaving effect. In this case, we'll be creating a fictitious product label for baking soda and we'll be introducing all of the elements of the final image before we move on to the next section.

1 Create a new file named SODA1.TIF. In the dialog box that now appears, specify a file size of 600 × 800 pixels at 72 dpi in the RGB mode. If the Info palette is not currently visible, choose Windows➡Show Info.

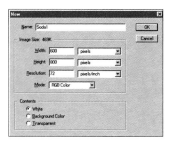

As with many of the techniques in this book, the Info palette is relied upon quite substantially to provide basic information about the current tool: its position in the image window; the color values of underlying pixels; and in many cases, size, distance, and angle of rotation information when applicable. The Info palette also gives you control over the units that it displays. In this technique, several of the steps specify operations with specific values that you must use in order to precisely produce the desired outcome. Therefore, you will want to make sure that the palette is visible at all times.

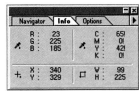

In this case, the Info palette should be used to properly place the cursor at its initial position, which the palette displays in its lower left quadrant. To specify different units, simply click the plus symbol to gain access to the units submenu and select the units you desire.

It is important to note that the final size of selections are always specified in terms of width and height values. This convention is used to accommodate situations where it is necessary to drag beyond the image window to define the appropriate selection. In these cases, the position of the cursor is not reported once it resides outside the image window because that information is no longer relevant. The width and height values of the selection, however, are still displayed in

2 Set the foreground color to red (R:255 G:0 B:0) and then set the background color to orange (R:253 G:108 B:0). Place the cursor at pixel location 70,70. Using the Elliptical Marquee tool, hold the Shift key and drag out a circular selection with a size of **460 × 460** pixels. Holding the Shift key links the width and height dimensions of Marquee selections so that symmetric selections are guaranteed.

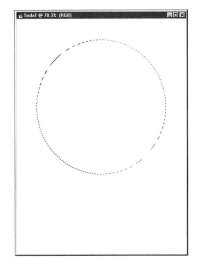

continues

continued

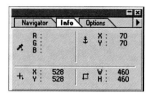

the lower right quadrant using the same units specified by the user for reporting pixel locations. This will become more clear in Step 7 when you will be required to define an elliptical selection by dragging the cursor beyond the image window.

3 Invert the selection and then fill the selection with the background color. Create a new layer (Layer 1) and then invert the selection once more. Now choose Edit➡Stroke (Width: 10 pixels, Location: Outside, Opacity: 100%) and then deselect the selection.

Also, note that the Info palette displays the initial start position of a selection in the upper right quadrant as the selection is being defined. The upper right quadrant is often used to display context-specific information that varies from one operation to the next.

In this case, the Stroke command was convenient but cannot always be used since a 16-pixel stroke width is the maximum. A more general approach could have been implemented using the selection tools to select the region and then fill it, which is the approach that we will use to create the inner red ring of the target symbol in the next step.

4 Using the Elliptical Marquee tool, place the cursor at pixel location (90,90) and drag out a circular selection with a pixel size of 420 × 420. Now place the cursor at pixel location (150,150). Hold the (Option)[Alt] key and drag out another selection with a pixel size of 300 × 300. Now fill the selection with the foreground color and then deselect the selection.

By holding the (Option)[Alt] key, notice that the second selection was automatically subtracted from the first. This is one of many convenient hot key

continues

continued

controls that will be used in this technique to quickly define composite selections as we move along. I've found these hot keys to be tremendous time-savers and highly recommend that you take the time to commit them to memory.

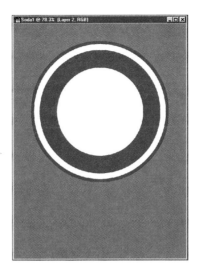

5 Create a new layer (Layer 2) and then set the foreground color to dark blue (R:36 G:0 B:128). Using the Rectangular Marquee tool, place the cursor at pixel location (20,20), and drag out a selection with a width and height of 560 × 760 pixels. Choose Edit➥Stroke (Width: 16 pixels, Location: Inside, Opacity: 100%). Now deselect the Selection.

6 Using the Type tool, enter the text Baking Soda. I used Haettenschweiler Bold at 120 points. Photoshop automatically places the text onto a new layer and names it Layer 3. Center the text in the lower portion of the image and then merge down Layer 3 with Layer 2.

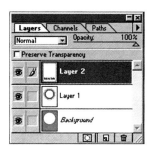

7 Create a new layer (Layer 3) and then set the foreground color to yellow (R:255 G:222 B:0). Using the Elliptical Marquee tool, place the cursor at pixel location (0,250) and drag out a selection with a width and height of 900 × 500 pixels. It may be necessary to zoom out the view to accomplish this dimension because you'll have to drag the cursor beyond the borders of the image window. Notice the absence of position information in the lower left and upper right quadrants of the Info palette as the selection is dragged out beyond the image window to its final size.

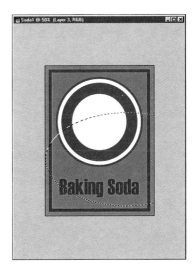

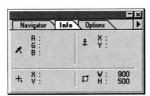

8 With the Elliptical Marquee tool still selected, place the cursor inside the selection and then move the selection to the left until the Info palette displays a relative pixel position of (-55,0). In this case, the Info palette dynamically displays the amount of the displacement as the move operation is implemented to help you complete the task correctly.

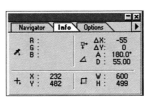

9 Place the cursor at pixel location (0,350). Using the Elliptical Marquee tool, hold the (Option)[Alt] key and drag out another selection with a width and height of 900 × 650 pixels. With the Elliptical Marquee tool still selected, place the cursor inside the selection and move it to the left until the Info palette displays a relative pixel position of (-10,0). Now fill the selection with the foreground color and then deselect the selection.

In this case, the selection is moved to the left to ensure that the subtracted area of the second selection extends slightly beyond the image window. This ensures that the lower edge of the ribbon has a smooth transition into the left edge of the image window.

10 Create a layer transparency selection from **Layer 1**. Save the selection to a new channel (**Channel #4**). Make Channel #4 active and then rename the channel **Element 1**. Repeat these operations for **Layer 2** to create a new channel named **Element 2** and for **Layer 3** to create a new channel named **Element 3**.

Editing the Yellow Ribbon

At this point, we basically have all the image elements in place. We've also saved selections based on the layer transparencies that will enable us to quickly isolate specific regions of the image based on the geometries of the individual image elements. These selections will be needed when we begin to produce the weaving effect. By saving these selections now, we are free to alter the transparencies of the image elements without creating problems down the road. This will become more clear in future steps when we complete the weaving operations. At this point, we will now move on to alter the transparency of the yellow ribbon. As you will soon see, this actually makes the final effect look very impressive because underlying elements will partially show through the ribbon as it passes seamlessly over them.

1 Create a new channel (Channel #7). Photoshop will automatically make Channel #7 active and visible. Photoshop will also make all other channels invisible, and the image window will be filled solidly with the color black.

2 Using the Rectangular Marquee tool, place the cursor at pixel location (0,0) and drag out a selection with a width and height of 5 × 800 pixels. Switch to the default colors and then fill the selection with the foreground color. Now deselect the selection. At this point, the image window should be black with a white vertical strip along the left edge. Using the Rectangular Marquee tool, place the cursor at pixel location (0,0) and drag out a selection having a width and height of 10 × 800 pixels. Choose Edit➥Define Pattern and then deselect the selection. Now choose Edit➥Fill (Use: Pattern, Opacity: 100%, Mode: Normal). This fills the entire image window with alternating vertical stripes of solid white and black.

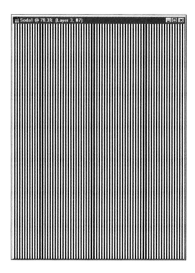

3 Choose Filter➧Blur➧Gaussian Blur (Radius: 1.0) and then select the Gradient tool from the toolbox. In the Gradient Tool Options palette, reset the tool and then choose Cancel when prompted. Now select the Foreground to Transparent option in the Gradient field. Switch the foreground and background colors. Place the cursor at pixel location (100,400) and drag a horizontal gradient out beyond the image window to a final distance of 700 pixels. Use the information displayed in the upper right quadrant of the Info palette to place the gradient accurately.

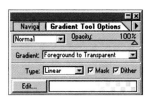

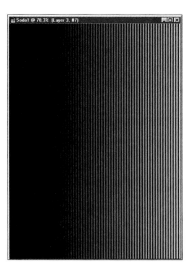

Notice the effect that the delete operation had on the pixels in the selection. In this case, they were modified based on the grayscale values of the mask in Channel #7 instead of the borders of the active selection. This is obvious because many of the pixels in the selection region were effected by different amounts. It is important to note that selections and masks are really one and the same. A selection is essentially a special case of a mask. For example, using the Marquee tool to define a selection is equivalent to painting a black mask with white pixels that define the same region as the selection border. It's that simple.

4 Load the selection from Channel #7. Photoshop applies a selection border based on a 50% threshold of the pixels in the mask. Now make the RGB channel active. With Layer 3 still active, press Delete to add transparent regions to the ribbon and then deselect the selection. In the Layers palette, place Layer 3 directly above the Background layer.

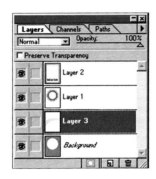

Creating the Weaving Effect

We're now ready to produce the weaving effect, but before we begin, I'd like to take a moment to present the general approach that we'll be implementing. The first goal of our approach will be to isolate all of the intersection regions between the element to be weaved and the other elements in the image. The resulting selection will then be edited even further to isolate only those regions of intersection where the ribbon is to pass above the other elements in the image. This selection will then be used to copy those regions of the ribbon above the other image elements in the stack, which is what will finally produce the weaving effect. This approach is much less complicated than it sounds. With the help of hot key controls, these operations can be implemented in a matter of seconds. Let's begin!

I Make sure that the Channels palette is open. Delete Channel #7 and make sure that the RGB channel is active. Hold (Command)[Control] and click the Element 1 channel to load it as a selection. Now hold (Command+Shift)[Control+Shift] and click the Element 2 channel to add it to the current selection. Choose Select➡Modify➡Expand (1 Pixel) to prevent edge defects that can otherwise occur in the final selection. Now hold (Command+Shift+Option) [Control+Shift+Alt] and click the Element 3 channel to intersect it with the current selection. Save the resulting selection to a new channel (Channel #7). Make Channel #7 active and then rename the channel to Intersections. Now make the RGB channel active.

It is important to note that the hot key controls used in this step are equally valid when working with transparency selections in the Layers palette. In fact, we could have created the selection saved in the Intersections channel from layer transparencies except for the fact that the yellow ribbon is no longer completely opaque. As a result, errors would have been introduced into the final selection. This is seen more clearly by comparing the corresponding masks of the two methods. Notice that the mask created from layer transparency does not solidly isolate the intersection regions in the same way as the mask from the Intersections channel. This is why we saved the layer transparency selections to channels in Step 10.

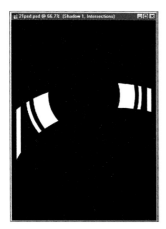

2 Deselect the selection. Using the Rectangular Marquee tool, place the cursor at pixel location (50,250) and drag out a selection with a width and height of 200 × 250 pixels. Now place the cursor at pixel location (550,250). Hold the Shift key and drag out another selection with a width and height of 50 × 130 pixels. Save the selection to a new channel (Channel #8). Now hold (Command+Shift+Option) [Control+Shift+Alt] and click the Intersections channel. We have now isolated the specific intersection regions of the ribbon that will be copied to a higher level in the stack of the Layers palette.

3 With Layer 3 still active, use the clipboard to copy the contents of the selection to a new layer (Layer 4). In the Layers palette, move Layer 4 to the top of the stack. The ribbon now appears to weave above the other image elements, but the image still looks flat, so we'll move on to add drop shadows that give the image some depth.

4 Make Layer 1 active. Now create a layer drop shadow named Shadow 1. Repeat these operations using the same naming convention to create layer drop shadows for Layers 2, 3, and 4. All of the necessary shadows should now be in place, but the Shadow 1 and Shadow 4 layers are casting shadows incorrectly onto the portion of the ribbon element that resides on Layer 1. Therefore, they must be trimmed to properly complete the effect. Also, please refer to the Basics section to review the prescribed method for creating drop shadows.

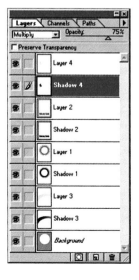

5 Make the Shadow 4 Layer active. Now switch to the Channels palette. Hold (Command)[Control] and click Channel #8 to load it as a selection. Hold (Command+Shift+Option) [Control+Shift+Alt] and click the Intersections channel. Press Delete to trim the unwanted portions of the Shadow 4 layer. Switch back to the Layers palette and make the Shadow 1 layer active. Press delete once again and the image is now complete. Now select Layer➟Flatten Image.

Chapter 4

Vignettes, Borders, and Backgrounds

Many of the techniques of this book present methods for cleaning up, colorizing, and otherwise improving the appearance of existing images, without changing their original composition. Even after you've implemented operations to improve the appearance of an image, there's a lot that can still be done to present the image in a more interesting and professional manner using vignettes, borders, and backgrounds. This is especially true when working with portrait-type images.

A vignette is characterized by the gradual fading of an image to a background along a geometric shape, such as an oval or square. Photographers used to produce vignetted images long before the existence of Photoshop, which now makes it possible to easily produce other border effects as well. With the use of multiple layers, channels, and layer masks, these edge effects can easily be implemented with greater flexibility that produces a high-quality result without permanently altering the underlying pixels of the original image.

In this technique, we'll make use of vignettes, borders, and backgrounds to enhance the presentation of more than one image to produce several final images. We'll begin by first producing a vignette in the simplest manner possible using not much more than a feathered selection. We'll then move on to enhance the vignetted image with the addition of a border and an abstract background—only the first of two vignetting examples that this technique presents.

After we've completed the first example, we'll move on to the second example in which we'll implement a totally different approach to produce a vignette for a different image. More specifically, we'll follow an approach that makes use of a channel and layer mask to provide more control over the final appearance of the image. The use of these features also provides more flexibility to make changes and adjustments as we move along. After we complete the second image, we'll then move on to implement some additional operations to present the second image in a more interesting and natural manner.

Creating Vignettes with Feathered Selections

One of the quickest and easiest ways to create a vignette is with the use of a feathered selection; we'll use one in the shape of an oval to produce a vignette around the sailor in the sample image of this section. In this case, our goal will be to produce the vignette to help center the viewer's attention on the head of the sailor. Therefore, we'll follow a more complex approach to make the sailor's head protrude out of the simple vignette that we produce. But that's not all; we'll also add a border, a background, and some artistic effects that dramatically increase the visual interest of the final image.

1 Open the file named SAILOR.TIF. This is the image that we wish to vignette. We'll create a vignette around the sailor and discard the remainder of the original image. In fact, we'll start by creating a composite selection in the next several steps. Once this selection is complete, we'll then use it to create the vignette for the final image.

2 Select the Elliptical Marquee tool from the toolbox. Place the cursor at pixel location (130,480) and drag out a selection to (960,1150). Now choose Select➡Feather (Radius: 8 pixels) and then save the selection to a new channel (Channel #4). Deselect the selection.

Channel #4 now contains the selection that defines the basic shape of the vignette, but this selection must be modified to include the remainder of the

continues

continued

head that protrudes outside the border of the oval. We'll move along to implement this modification in the next two steps.

In this case, our goal was to select all the pixels of the sky. Because the sky is relatively bright and because all the pixels that define the sky are predominantly blue, it's reasonable to expect that this region will stand out in the Blue channel. As a result, it's also reasonable to expect that the region can be selected more easily and quickly with the Magic Wand tool than what would have otherwise been possible in the RGB channel. In this case, the Magic Wand tool worked very well. Nevertheless, we also had to expand the selection that did not extend right up to the edge of the sailor's head. In fact, this is a common consequence of antialiased edges that must be dealt with when using the Magic Wand tool. As you can see, this characteristic can be overcome quite easily with the

continues

3 In the Channels palette, make the Blue channel active and then select the Magic Wand tool from the toolbox. In the Magic Wand Options palette, reset the tool and then specify a value of 64 in the Tolerance field. Now define a selection by clicking pixel location (940,730). It's important to note that you'll most likely get an acceptable selection by clicking any location in the immediate region of the pixel location specified. If necessary, use the Zoom tool to zoom into the immediate area so that you can define the selection from the exact pixel location specified and then choose View➡Fit on Screen to zoom the view back out. Now choose Select➡Modify➡Expand (2 pixels) and then choose Select➡Feather (Radius: 4 pixels).

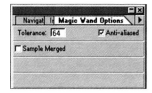

continued

Expand command. In some cases, you might have to use the Contract command instead.

4 Make the RGB channel active **and then** invert the selection. Select the Rectangular Marquee tool from the toolbox. Now place the cursor at pixel location (360,280). Hold the (Option+Shift)[Alt+Shift] keys and drag out a selection to (960,840) to intersect it with the current selection and obtain the selection that is shown.

Now hold the (Command+Shift)[Control+Shift] keys and load the selection from Channel #4 to add it to the current selection. We now have the composite selection that we need to create the vignette that we desire.

At this point, the vignette is complete, but the sailor appears to be having a bad hair day. Therefore, we'll want to implement a few touch-ups before moving on.

5 With the selection still active, use the clipboard to copy the contents of the selection to a new layer (Layer 1) and then rename the layer to Vignette. Now choose Layer➡Transform➡Numeric and then specify a relative pixel position of (+62,-120). This centers the vignette over the background in the image window, but we still need to fill the background with a solid color for it to properly show up. Make the Background layer active. Switch to the default colors and then switch the foreground and background colors. Now fill the layer with the foreground color.

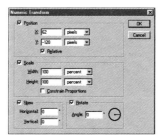

6 Select the Eraser tool from the toolbox. In the Brushes palette, select the New Brush command from the palette pullout menu. In the Brush Options dialog box that now appears, adjust the settings to (Diameter: 25 pixels, Hardness: 0%, Spacing: 25 pixels). This brush will now be used by the Eraser tool that we'll use to eliminate the hair that is sticking out of the sailor's head on the right. We'll now use this brush to edit the vignette.

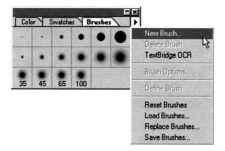

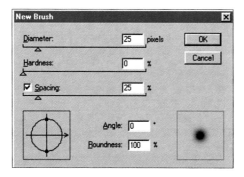

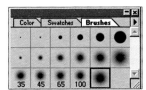

In the next few steps, we'll add a border to the image before moving along to introduce a background image. In this case, we'll have to edit the new background to improve its appearance so that it doesn't detract from the vignette.

7 Make the Vignette layer active and then use the Eraser tool to eliminate the hair sticking out of the right side of the sailor's head. This is definitely an improvement, but a lot can still be done to improve the presentation of the vignette.

The borders of this selection define the path along which we'll place the border to be introduced. However, we won't be using the Edit➡Stroke command as you might have anticipated because this command can be used only to draw lines along the edge of the existing selection. Instead, we'll convert the existing selection to a path so that we can use the Stroke Path command that is offered in the Paths palette pullout menu. This command provides more capability. In fact, we'll

8 Select the Rectangular Marquee tool from the toolbox and define a selection from pixel location (40,40) to (1160, 1560).

continues

continued

configure this command to draw a more interesting border by using the Paintbrush tool in conjunction with a custom brush. This will all become more clear as we proceed, and we'll start by loading the Custom brush that we want the border to be created with.

9 Select the Paintbrush tool from the toolbox. In the Brushes palette, select the Load Brushes command from the palette pull-out menu and then select the file named BRUSH.ABR located on the CD-ROM. This appends a new brush to the Brushes palette. In the Brushes palette, select the new brush that appears. Now select the Brush Options command also located in the palette pullout menu. In the dialog box that now appears, adjust the Spacing to 100%.

In this case, it's important to note that there's nothing special about this brush. It's simply a custom brush that I defined for use with this image, but you may use other brushes to produce borders that have a different appearance. Instead, Adobe provides several additional brushes with Photoshop that you can use. However, these brushes don't show up in the default selection that the Brushes palette displays. Therefore, you'll have to explicitly load them off the Photoshop application CD-ROM in the same way that you just loaded the brush off the CD-ROM provided with this book.

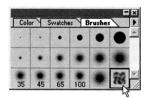

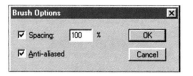

10 Switch to the default colors. In the Paths palette, choose the Make Work Path command from the palette pullout menu. In the dialog box that now appears, specify a value of 2.0 pixels in the Tolerance field. Now select the Stroke Path command from the palette pullout menu. In the dialog box that appears, specify the Paintbrush as the tool. Now choose the Turn Off Path command from the palette pullout menu.

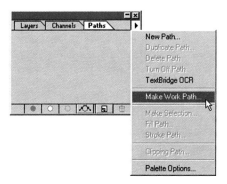

11 Make the Background layer active and then open the file named BOATS.TIF. Choose Select➥All and then use the clipboard to copy the contents of the selection to a new layer (Layer 1) in the working image (SAILOR.TIF). Now close the BOATS.TIF file without saving and then merge down Layer 1 with the Background layer.

In the next several steps, , we'll implement modifications to the appearance of the new background image, which currently distracts instead of enhancing the vignette.

12 Choose Image➥Adjust➥Desaturate and then choose Image➥Adjust➥Hue/Saturation. In the dialog box that now appears, turn on the Color option and then adjust the settings to (Hue: 40, Saturation: 30, Lightness: -30). Now choose Filter➥Artistic➥Palette Knife (Stroke Size: 10, Stroke Detail: 3, Softness: 6).

By desaturating the background, we eliminated the multiple colors that were present so that we could then use the Hue/Saturation controls to quickly create a sepia-toned image. By doing this, the colors of the vignetted image now show up more prominently so that the viewer is more properly focused on the sailor. However, there's still more work that needs to be done. In the next several steps, we'll implement some additional operations to soften the background image, as well as to darken it. These operations will help to further draw the attention of the viewer to the sailor.

13 Duplicate the Background layer. With the duplicate layer (Background copy) now active, choose Filter➡Blur➡Gaussian Blur (Radius: 10.0 pixels). Now adjust the layer opacity to 70% and then merge down the duplicate layer with the Background layer.

14 Create a new layer (Layer 1) and then select the Gradient tool from the toolbox. In the Gradient Tool Options palette, reset the tool and then select Cancel when prompted. Specify Transparent to Foreground in the Gradient field and then switch to the default colors. Now define a gradient from the top center to the bottom center of the image window and then adjust the layer opacity to 65%. Merge down Layer 1 with the Background layer. At this point, the background image looks great. We'll now move on to implement some additional modifications to create a more artistic look for the image.

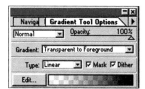

15 Duplicate the Vignette layer. With the duplicate layer (Vignette copy) now active, choose Image➡Adjust➡Desaturate and then choose Filter➡Artistic➡Colored Pencil (Pencil Width: 4, Stroke Pressure: 12, Paper Brightness: 50). Change the layer apply mode to Multiply and then adjust the layer opacity to 70%. Now make the Vignette layer active and then choose Brightness/Contrast (Brightness: +35, Contrast: +35). At this point, the image is complete. If you want, choose Layer➡Flatten Image and save the file.

Creating Vignettes with Channels and Layer Masks

In the fist example, we used a feathered selection to quickly create the vignette that we produced. Although this method was
simple, it doesn't provide much flexibility for making modifications. Therefore, we'll explore a more advanced approach to
demonstrate how you can build more flexibility into the development process. The new approach will also provide us with more
flexibility for controlling exactly how the edge of vignette fades
(transitions) to the surrounding region.

1 Open the file named BOY.TIF. This is the second image that we
wish to vignette.

2 Create a new layer named Paper, and then set the foreground
color to off-white (R: 240 G: 230 B: 210). Now fill the layer with
the foreground color. Choose Filter➡Noise➡Add Noise
(Amount: 30, Distribution: Gaussian, Monochromatic: Checked)
and then choose Filter➡Blur➡Gaussian Blur (Radius: 2.0 pixels).
Now choose Filter➡Blur➡Motion Blur (Distance: 40, Angle: 45
degrees) and then choose Image➡Adjust Brightness/Contrast
(Brightness: -30, Contrast: +30). This creates a pleasing background with slight color variations upon which we'll now place a
vignetted version of the image.

*At this point, we'll move on to
prepare a mask that we'll then
apply to the image as a layer
mask, which will produce the
vignetting effect. As already
mentioned, this approach provides a greater degree of flexibility for implementing changes
as we proceed. In fact, the
image of the boy will not be
permanently altered by the*

continues

continued

mask, which we'll be able to discard at any time to reveal the original image in its entirety. We'll also be able to move the image within the borders of the vignette to recenter it. This new approach is also more advanced because it will provide us with more control over the way that the vignetted image fades or transitions to surrounding regions of the image.

3 Select the Elliptical Marquee tool from the toolbox and place the cursor at pixel location (200,250). Now drag out a selection with a width and height of 800 × 1100 pixels. Choose Select➡Feather (Radius: 16 pixels) and then save the selection to a new channel (Channel #4). Deselect the selection. Now make Channel #4 active so that the corresponding mask is displayed in the image window.

4 Select the Magic Wand tool from the toolbox. In the Magic Wand Options palette, reset the tool and specify a value of 4 in the Tolerance field. Now define a new selection by sampling the center of the solid white region of the mask. Choose Select➡Feather (Radius: 16 pixels) and then invert the selection. Hold (Command+Option+Shift)[Control+Alt+Shift] and click Channel #4 in the Channels palette to load the channel and intersect it with the current selection. This creates a new selection that isolates the border of the mask, and we'll now use it to edit the mask in Channel #4.

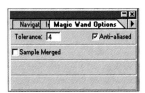

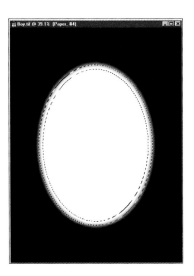

5 With the composite selection still active, choose Filter➡Noise➡Add Noise (Amount: 200, Distribution: Uniform, Monochromatic: Checked). Now deselect the selection.

Because the active selection and the mask both had feathered edges before the intersection operation was performed, there is a smooth transition of the noise to both the white interior and black exterior regions of the mask. We're now ready to apply the mask to create the vignette effect.

It's important to note that Photoshop does not allow transformations to be applied to the Background layer. This is why we made a duplicate of the background before we centered the boy within the vignette.

At this point, the image looks great and the best part is that we're not locked into the final appearance because we can either recenter the portrait within the vignette or even discard the mask to eliminate the vignette and obtain the original appearance of the image. This is often a convenient feature, but we won't be taking further advantage of it in this technique, and therefore we'll flatten the image in the next step to simplify the operations of the remaining steps.

6 Load the selection from Channel #4 and then make the RGB channel active. With the Paper layer still active, choose Layer➡Add Layer Mask➡Hide Selection. At this point, the selection has been applied as a layer mask so that the Background image now shows through the Paper layer. However, the image of the boy is not properly centered. To correct this, duplicate the background layer. With the duplicate layer (Background copy) now active, choose Layer➡Transform➡Numeric. In the dialog box that now appears, specify a relative pixel position of (-50,+100). The vignette is now complete!

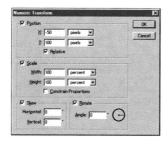

7 Choose Layer➥Flatten Image and then select the Rectangular Marquee tool from the toolbox. Place the cursor at pixel location (40,40) and then drag out a selection to (1160,1560). Now choose Select➥Feather (Radius: 2 pixels) and then invert the selection. Set the foreground color to off-white (R: 240 G: 240 B: 230) and then fill the selection with the foreground color. The vignetted image is now complete and it looks excellent. At this point, we'll move on to complete a third image using the vignetted image that we just developed.

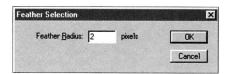

Image Presentation

1 If you want, you may use the vignetted image that I produced instead of your own by first closing your image and then opening the file named 04FINAL1.JPG. Choose Select➡All and then copy the contents of the selection to the clipboard. Now open the file named PHOTOS.PSD. I prepared this file so that we could use it to present our vignetted image in a more interesting way.

Now that you're an expert in producing vignetting effects, let's move on to explore one more method of image presentation. In this section, we'll implement some additional operations to display the image of the previous section in a more natural setting. More specifically, we'll present the image with several other images that appear to be strewn across a flat surface. As I'm sure you'll agree, these additional operations make a big difference!

2 With the PHOTOS.PSD file and the Background layer both active, choose Edit➡Paste to place the contents of the clipboard to a new layer (Layer 1). Now close the file from which the vignetted image was copied before moving on.

At this point, the pasted image of the boy is covering the entire image window and all the other photos except for the one that resides on the Photo 1 layer above the pasted image layer (Layer 1) in the Layers palette. In the next step, we will transform the pasted image to its final size, position, and orientation so that the photos on the Background layer become partially visible once again.

3 Choose Layer➡Transform➡Numeric. In the dialog box that now appears, specify a relative pixel position of (-10,60) and scaling factors of 70% for both the width and height. Finally, specify a rotation angle of +10 degrees. With Layer 1 still active, create a layer drop shadow. At this point, the vignetted image fits in quite well with the other photos of the image, but in order to complete the image, we need to de-emphasize the other photos in the image to help draw the eye more immediately to the vignetted image that we want to show off. We'll accomplish this by using some of the same concepts that were presented with the first example image of this technique.

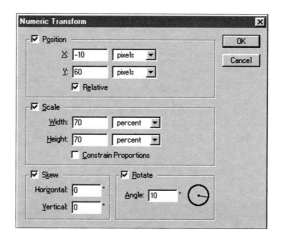

4 Duplicate the Background layer. With the duplicate layer (Background copy) now active, choose Filter➡Blur Gaussian Blur (Radius: 6.0 pixels) and then adjust the layer opacity to 60%. Merge down the duplicate layer with the Background layer. Now duplicate the Photo 1 layer. With the duplicate layer (Photo 1 copy) now active, choose Filter➡Blur➡Gaussian Blur (Radius: 6.0 pixels) and then adjust the layer opacity to 60%. Now merge down the duplicate layer with the Photo 1 layer. This improves the appearance quite well. At this point, we'll move on to the final step in which we'll introduce a gradient to complete the image.

5 Make the Background layer active and then create a new layer (Layer 1). Now select the Gradient tool from the toolbox. In the Gradient Tool Options palette, reset the tool and then select Cancel when prompted. Specify Transparent to Foreground in the Gradient field and then switch to the default colors. Now define a gradient from the bottom right corner to the top left corner of the image window and then adjust the layer opacity to 80%. Choose Layer➥Flatten Image. Congratulations! The image is complete and looks fantastic.

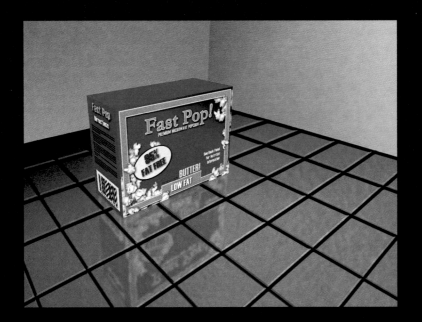

Chapter 5

Introducing Artificial Perspective for Emphasis

Other chapters in this book show how to accurately place a three-dimensional object into a background by matching the existing perspective of the image to produce a final representation that looks very natural. Perspective is an extremely powerful tool for producing realism, but perspective can also be used in just the opposite way. In fact, perspective is often exaggerated for the purpose of creating a sense of emphasis. By exaggerating the perspective of an object or a scene, it is often possible to convey a sense of power, strength, and importance. In this chapter, we'll produce a completely artificial scene with exaggerated perspective to add emphasis to a commercial box of microwave popcorn.

In this example, we're completely free to define the perspective that will be used since we won't be working from an existing background image. As a result, we are also free to implement a very effective shortcut that will enable us to simulate perspective in the vertical direction with a single operation and without using a third vanishing point. This turns out to be of extreme benefit, because vertical perspective is often not very pronounced and would have required that a vanishing point be placed far from the center of the image. By avoiding this circumstance, we are also eliminating the need to expand the image canvas by a significant amount, which ultimately enables us to work more quickly and efficiently. Nevertheless, the addition of vertical perspective will also complicate the placement of reflection images below the box.

Placing the Construction Lines of the Box

In this section, we'll define the vanishing points and place the construction lines that define the outlines of the box that we'll be creating. We'll then introduce some exaggerated vertical perspective before moving onto the next section, where we'll begin placing the construction lines of the tiled surface upon which the box will sit.

1 Create a new file with a size of 1850 × 900 pixels at 72 dpi. Switch to the default colors and make sure that the Info palette is visible.

2 Choose View➡Show Rulers and then place a vertical guide at pixel location 20 and another at 1800. Now place a horizontal guide at 10 pixels. These guides define right and left vanishing points that will be used to construct the scene.

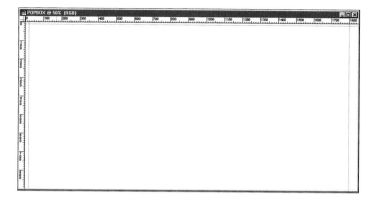

3 Create a new layer named Construction Lines. Set the fore-ground color to red (R:255 G:0 B:0) and then select the Line tool from the toolbox. In the Line Tool Options palette, reset the tool and then specify a width of 5 pixels. In this example, accurate placement of the individual construction lines is important to ensure that everything is correctly aligned once the construction lines are all in place. Therefore, we'll make additional use of guides.

Place a vertical guide at 535 pixels. If necessary, use the Zoom tool to zoom in on the view to make sure that the guide is placed at the exact pixel location specified. Now place a horizontal guide at pixel location 220 and another at 535. Once again, zoom in on the view if necessary to ensure that the guides are placed at the exact pixel locations. Enter the View menu and make sure that a check mark appears in front of the Snap to Guides command. If not, select it. Now choose View➥Fit on Screen to view the entire image canvas. Draw the leading edge of the box from pixel location (535,220) to (535,535). Now draw perspective lines from both the left and right vanishing points to the top and bottom ends of the leading edge.

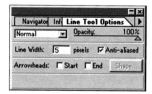

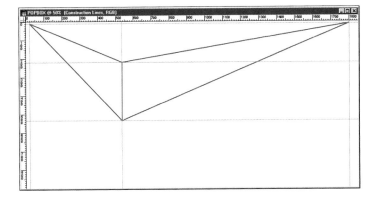

Before moving on, it is important to note that the initial position of the leading edge was determined somewhat arbitrarily with the help of a few guiding principles. When placing the leading edge of the box, keep in mind that the apparent elevation of the final view is determined by the relative position of the leading edge with respect to the horizon. In our example, the leading edge was placed below the horizon to produce a final view from above, but it would have been perfectly acceptable to place the leading edge on the horizon or even above it to produce a view from the front as well as from below. The viewing angle is also affected by the right to left placement of the leading edge. In our example, the leading edge was placed closer to the left vanishing point to provide a more direct view of the front panel of the box. If we had desired a more direct view of the side panel, we would have placed the leading edge closer to the right vanishing point instead.

4 Let's now complete the box. Place a vertical guide at pixel location **450** and another at **880** to define the left and right edges of the box. Now place horizontal guides to accurately define the top and bottom intersection points of the vertical guides with the perspective lines that lead out to the vanishing points. You will have to zoom in on the view to place these correctly.

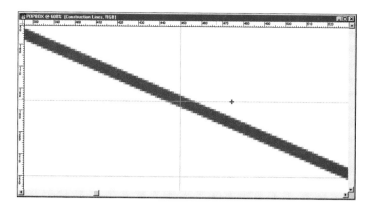

I placed a horizontal guide at pixel location 185 and another at 447 to define the intersection points of the left edge. I also placed a horizontal guide at pixel location 163 and another at 392 to define the intersection points of the right edge. Now you are ready to draw the lines that complete the box.

At this point, we have the basic framework of the box in place. In fact, the amount of perspective looks perfect for producing a completely natural scene! But our goal is somewhat different. We want to use perspective as a tool for adding emphasis to make the popcorn box of the final image appear as though it's practically jumping out into the third dimension! This will be accomplished by adding and slightly exaggerating perspective in the vertical dimension of the image using a shortcut that will enable us to avoid the use of a third vanishing point.

Choose View➡Fit on Screen to view the entire canvas. Place the cursor at pixel location (450,185) and draw a vertical line to (450,447) to complete the left edge and then draw perspective lines to the right vanishing point from both the top and bottom ends of the edge. Now place the cursor at (880,163) and draw a vertical line to (880,392) to complete the right edge and then draw perspective lines to the left vanishing point from both the top and bottom ends of the edge. Complete the box by drawing another vertical line from (770,144) to (770,344) to produce the back right edge.

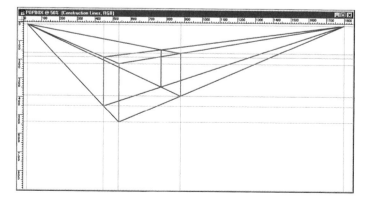

5 With the Construction Lines layer still active, choose Layers➡Transform➡Perspective. Now move the bottom right handle of the Transformation tool inward. As you slide the right handle over, use the information provided in the upper right quadrant of the Info palette to reproduce the same amount of skewing as shown. At this point, the lowest figure in the upper right quadrant should read -20.

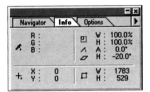

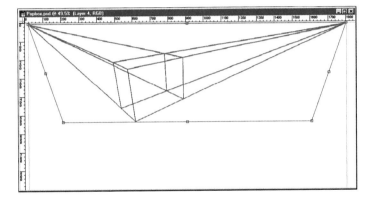

Now use the bottom center handle to achieve the correct balance of right and left skewing. As you move the handle to the left, use the information provided in the upper right quadrant of the Info palette to reproduce the same amount of balance as shown. Before accepting the modifications, the lowest figure in the upper right quadrant should read -24.5.

As you move the handles inward, the apparent view will change slightly, but notice the dramatic effect that even a small amount of vertical perspective has on the three-dimensional appearance of the box. The effect is quite impressive.

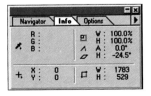

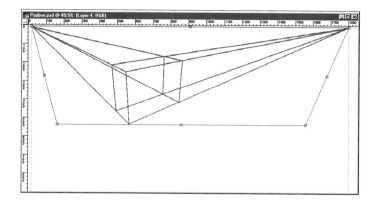

Placing the Construction Lines of the Tiled Surface

Now that the form of the box is defined, we can proceed to place the construction lines of the tiled surface. We'll place these additional lines in this section, and then we'll move on to the next section where we'll begin to add texture to the tiles to simulate a ceramic surface.

I Create a new layer named Tiles. Switch to the default colors. Using the Line tool, draw a line from the right vanishing point that passes down the centerline of the box's bottom surface and then over to the extreme left end of the image canvas. Now draw another line from the right vanishing point that passes directly in front of the box and then over to the extreme left edge of the image canvas. These lines are the first of several that will be used to construct a tiled base upon which the commercial product will appear to reside.

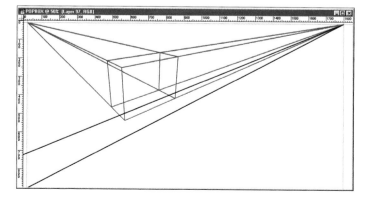

2 Now draw a line from the left vanishing point that passes just in front of the left panel of the box and then down to the bottom edge of the image canvas. Now draw another line from the left vanishing point such that it appears to form a square tile under the leading edge of the box.

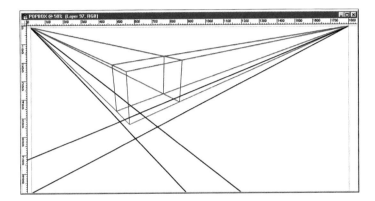

3 Continue to draw additional lines from the left vanishing point to form a chain of square tiles that extends approximately 2.5 tiles beyond each end of the box as shown.

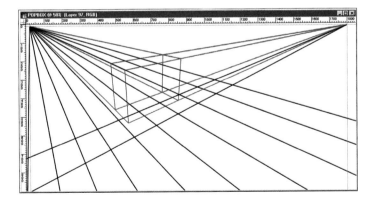

4 Now draw lines from the right vanishing point to produce an entire grid of tiles that appears to fill the entire foreground of the image, extending 2.5 tiles behind the left edge of the box as shown.

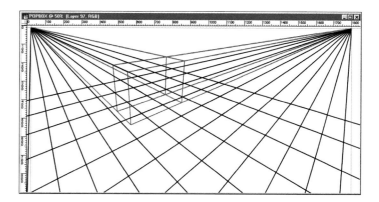

5 Using the Polygon Lasso tool, select the areas of the image not covered by the grid and press Delete to remove everything from those regions. Invert the selection and then save the selection to a new channel (Channel #4). Now load the layer transparency selection from the Tiles layer and then save the selection to a new channel (Channel #5). Deselect the selection.

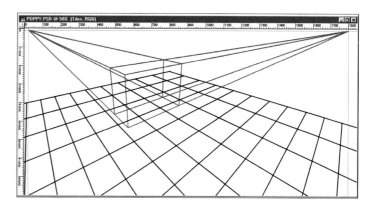

6 Make the Background layer active. Load the selection from Channel #4. Set the foreground color to bright blue (R:10 G:70 B:200) and then fill the selection with the foreground color.

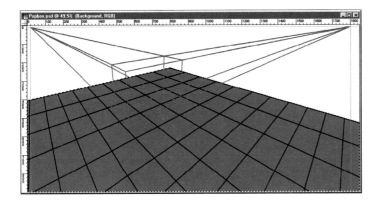

7 With the selection still active, choose Filter➡Add Noise (Amount: 12, Distribution: Gaussian, Monochromatic: Not Checked). Choose Filter➡Blur➡Gaussian Blur (Radius: 1.3 pixels). Now switch to the default colors. Select the Gradient tool. In the Gradient Tool Options palette, reset the tool and then select Cancel when prompted. Specify Transparent to Foreground in the Gradient field. While still working in the Gradient Options palette, change the apply mode to Multiply and adjust the gradient opacity slider to 70%. Now drag out a gradient from pixel location (730,550) to (770,260).

This darkens the area behind the box. In this example, we won't be adding any cast shadows into the final image so that the lighting scheme appears to be dominated by a strong ambient component. Nevertheless, we should still expect the area behind the box to be darker than other areas of the final image and the Gradient tool is a great way to produce this effect.

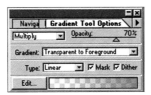

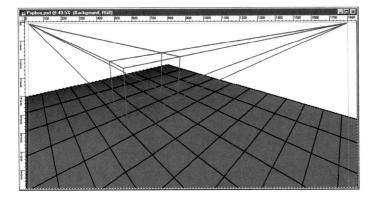

8 Choose Filter➡Artistic➡Plastic Wrap (Highlight Strength: 3, Detail: 15, Smoothness: 10). This generates a texture that simulates the soft, random roughness of ceramic tile. The Plastic Wrap filter adds highlights and creates the surface texture based on the amount of noise that was previously added in Step 7. Greater noise produces more roughness.

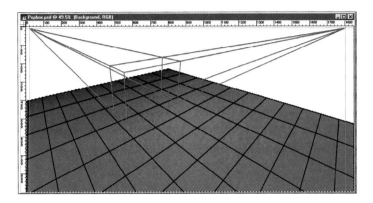

The blurred pixels will now be used by the Lighting Effects filter to create tile edges that look more three-dimensional with soft beveled edges. If the Magic Wand tool had not been used to clip the blurred edges, the Lighting Effects filter that is now going to be applied would have produced tile edges that were more rounded. This is something that you will have to experiment with to understand more clearly.

9 In the Channels palette, make Channel #5 active. Photoshop will automatically make Channel #5 visible and the corresponding mask will be displayed in the image window. Choose Filter➡Blur➡Gaussian Blur (Radius: 2.5 pixels). Select the Magic Wand tool. In the Magic Wand Options palette, reset the tool and then specify a tolerance of 16 pixels. Select a solid black area in the image window. Now choose Select➡Similar to include all solid black areas of the mask in the selection. Switch to the default colors and then press Delete. Deselect the selection.

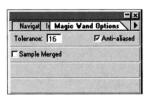

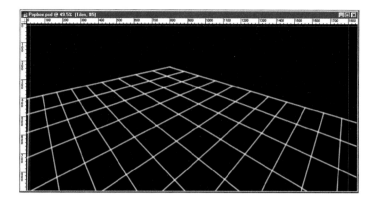

10 Make the RGB channel active. With the Background layer still active, choose Filter➡Render➡Lighting Effects and use the settings as shown. Be sure to Select Channel #5 in the Texture field. This adds highlights and shadows to the edges of the tiles and makes the grout lines appear to be recessed.

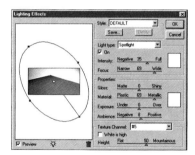

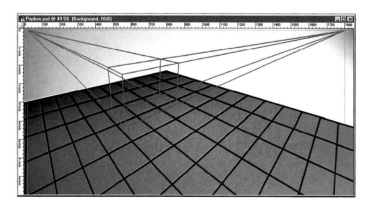

Creating the Back Walls

Now that the tiles are in place, we'll move on to create the back walls. In this case, there will be a right and a left back wall that need to be created, and we'll use the selection tools to isolate each region individually so that we can quickly paint these walls separately using the Gradient tool.

1 Load the selection from Channel #4 and then invert the selection. The selection now isolates the portion of the image above the tiled base. At this point, we'll add gradients to create a right and a left wall.

Before we begin, choose View→Snap to Guides. This will toggle off the snap feature of the existing guides so that they do not interfere with the ensuing operations. Select the Rectangular Marquee tool. Now hold the (Option)[Alt] key and subtract out the portion of the existing selection that falls to the left of the back corner of the tiled base. This isolates the upper right hand side of the image for creating the right back wall. This selection, however, still needs one slight modification.

Hold the (Option)[Alt] key and use the Polygon Lasso tool to subtract out a slight wedge from the left vertical border of the selection so that it now slants towards the right. The subtraction should be carried out so that the border slants at approximately the same angle as the back right edge of the red construction box. By performing this operation, we are maintaining consistency in the vertical perspective of the image. I have zoomed in on the view of the accompanying image so that you may see this more clearly. Before continuing, save the selection to a new channel (Channel #6).

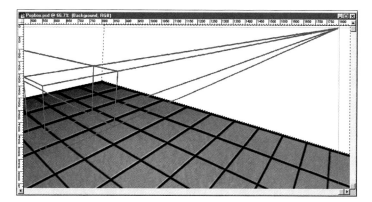

2 Switch to the default colors and then set the foreground color
to (R:120 G:120 B:120). Now select the Gradient tool. In the
Gradient Tool Options palette, reset the tool and select Cancel
when prompted. Specify Foreground to Background in the
Gradient field. Now drag out a gradient from the lower left corner to the upper right corner of the selection area. This creates
the back right wall. Now deselect the selection and use the Magic
Wand tool to select the solid white region in the upper left corner of the image. Drag out a gradient from the lower right corner to the upper left corner of the selection and then deselect
the selection. This creates the back left wall. Notice that the
adjoining edge of the two back walls is barely evident. This must
be corrected.

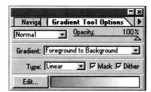

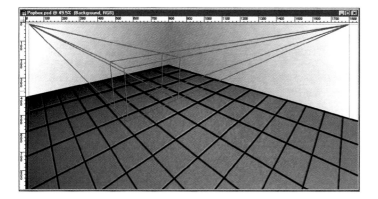

3 Load the selection from Channel #6. Choose Image➡Adjust➡
Brightness/Contrast (Brightness: 20, Contrast: 0). Now deselect
the selection and delete Channel #6. The adjoining edge is now
much more visible. By brightening the back left wall, we have also
provided a visual cue indicating lighting from the right.

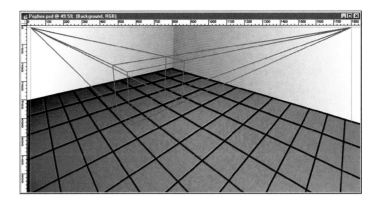

Introducing the Box

Now that the background elements are all in place, we can begin to place the panels of the box.

1 Open the file named POPBOX1.TIF. This file contains the front panel of the box. Choose Select➡All and copy the contents of the selection to the Clipboard. Close the file without saving. Now paste the contents of the Clipboard to the working image. Photoshop will automatically create a new layer and name it Layer 1. Move Layer 1 above all other layers in the Layers palette. The pasted image will now cover the entire image window and must be scaled down so that we can use it. Choose Layer➡Transform➡Numeric and scale the image by 60%.

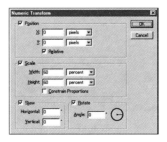

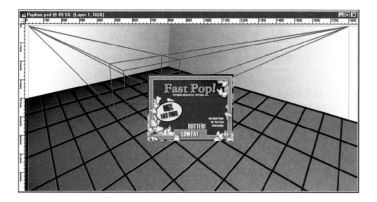

2 Zoom in on the view as much as possible while maintaining the view of both the front face of the construction box and the product label. Choose Layer➡Transform➡Distort and then use the handles to match the corners of the product label to the corners of the front face of the construction box.

3 Repeat Steps 1 and 2 using the image in the file named POP-BOX2.TIF to complete the left side panel of the box on a new layer named Layer 2. With the side panel in place, notice that the left edge of the box is not very pronounced. Choose Image➡Adjust➡Brightness/Contrast (Brightness: -40, Contrast: 0).

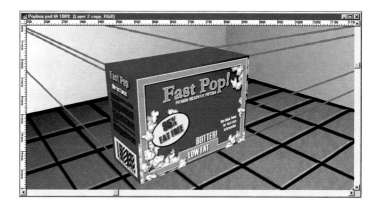

4 Now let's complete the top of the box. Create a new layer (Layer 3). Zoom in on the view and use the Polygon Lasso tool to trace out the outline of the box top. Use the Eyedropper tool to set the foreground color to the brightest blue on the front panel of the box and then fill the selection with the foreground color. Deselect the selection.

5 Now that all the panels of the box are in place, there are several things that can be done to correct any existing flaws that may exist. Start by making the Construction Lines layer invisible. This will make it easier for you to evaluate slight mismatches and other imperfections along the common edges where the individual panels of the box join. There are numerous ways to eliminate these. If corrections are implemented in your image, place them on a new layer named Edges.

Before moving on, make the Construction Lines layer visible once again. In the working image that accompanies this technique, the edges already look very clean, but there were a few small gaps where the background showed through. I then used the Line tool with a width of three pixels to draw lines along the common edges of the three panels using the same color used to create the top of the box. The Edges layer was then moved below all of the box panel layers in the Layers palette.

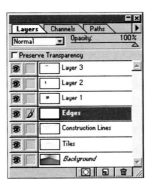

Introducing the Box Reflection

At this point, the box is complete, but there are several finishing touches that we must add in order to better integrate the box with its surroundings. The next several steps will show you how to add a realistic-looking reflection of the box to the tiled surface. In fact, we'll also apply a filter to the reflected image so that it simulates the natural contours of the tiled surface on which it appears.

With the addition of these lines, we now have the capability to place reflection images that are consistent with the vertical perspective of the box. No more construction lines will be added to the image. Choose View➡Hide Guides since they will no longer be required.

1 Make the Construction Lines layer active and set the foreground color to red (R:255 G:0 B:0). Now make Layers 1 through 3 and the Edges layer invisible. Choose View➡Snap to Guides to toggle on the snapping feature that was previously toggled off. Using the Line tool, add new construction lines that extend the right, left, and leading edges of the box down to the bottom edge of the image. Now draw a perspective line down to the leading edge to bound a region below the existing front panel of the box that approximately matches the size and height of that panel. Draw another perspective line from the left vanishing point to the same location on the leading edge. Now make all layers visible.

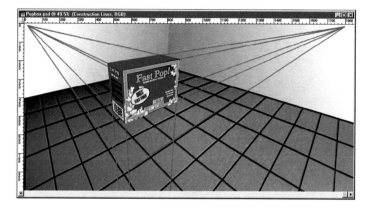

2 Make Layer 1 active and then duplicate the layer. Now move the duplicate layer (Layer 1 copy) above all other layers in the Layers palette. Choose Layer➡Transform➡Flip Vertical and then place the resulting image so that its upper left corner touches the lower right corner of the box.

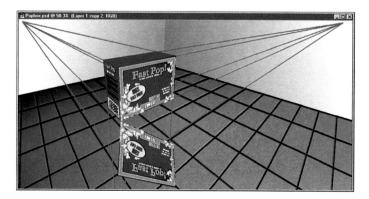

3 Choose Layer➡Transform➡Skew and use the handles to match the corners of the image to the corners defined by the newly placed construction lines.

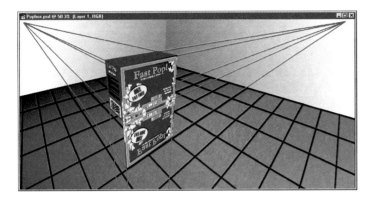

4 Repeat Steps 2 and 3 to complete the left panel reflection of the box as well. When repeating Step 2, use Layer 2 instead of Layer 1. The Layers palette should now contain an additional layer named Layer 2 copy, which should be placed at the top of the palette next to Layer 1.

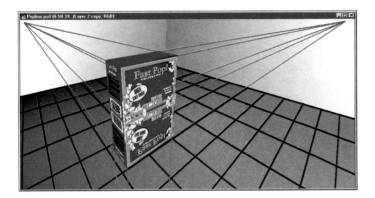

5 In the next step, the reflection images will be edited so that they fit in more appropriately with their surroundings. But before we move on, let's clean things up a little. With Layer 1 copy still active, link Layer 2 copy and then merge the linked layers. Rename the resulting layer **Box Reflection**. Now that the reflection is in place, it is also safe to merge all of the layers that form the geometry of the box. Make Layer 1 active and then link

Layers 2 and 3 with Layer 1. Also, link the Edges layer if it was created. Now merge the linked layers and rename the resulting layer **Popcorn Box.** Delete the Construction Lines layer. Now make the Tiles layer active and then merge down the active layer with the Background layer.

6 Make the Box Reflection layer active and adjust the layer opacity to 30%. Choose Filter➥Distort➥Ocean Ripple (Size: 15, Magnitude: 3). These values were chosen to reproduce distortions that best match the surface variations of the tile. Choose Filter➥Blur➥Gaussian Blur (Radius: 2.5). This softens the reflection and reduces detail that you would not expect to see in a reflection from ceramic tile. We now need to subtract the reflection from the grout lines before it is complete, but this will require that we first edit the mask in Channel #5.

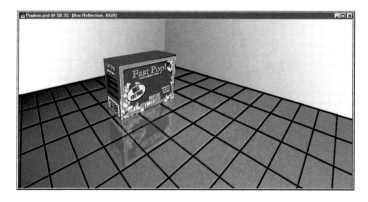

7 In the Channels palette, make Channel #5 active. Photoshop will automatically make Channel #5 visible and all other channels invisible. The image window will now display the mask as well. Select the Magic Wand tool. In the Magic Wand Options palette, set the Tolerance to 1. Now select a solid black area of the mask. Choose Select➥Similar and then invert the selection.

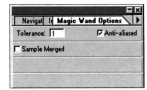

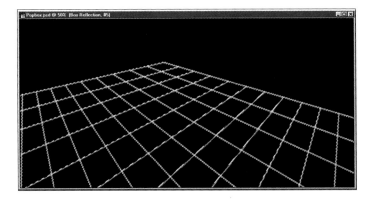

8 Make the RGB channel active. Photoshop will automatically make the RGB channel visible and Channel #5 invisible. With the Box Reflection layer still active, press Delete to subtract the regions of the reflection that fall above the grout lines. Now deselect the selection.

It is important to note that the selection that was just used is not the same selection that would have been obtained if we had loaded the channel as a selection and then inverted it. The corresponding mask of our selection contained only black and white pixels. In other words, we did not load the selection from Channel #5; we used it to create an independent selection with no interim values in the grayscale.

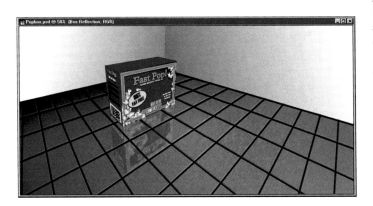

Adding the Finishing Touches

At this point the image is basically complete. Now that all of the image elements are properly in place, it is a good time to evaluate the overall lighting and make any corrections that are necessary. In this case, the upper left portion of the image seems a bit bright and detracts attention from the box. This must be corrected.

1 Make the Background layer active. Switch to the default colors and then select the Gradient tool. In the Gradient Tool Options palette, specify Foreground to Transparent and adjust the opacity slider to 70%. Now drag out a gradient from the upper left corner of the image to the bottom of the leading edge of the popcorn box. This really makes the box stand out!

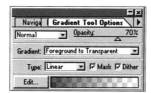

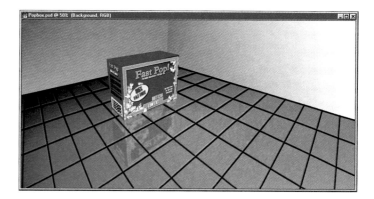

2 The image is now complete. Flatten the image and then use the Crop tool to remove excess space. When cropping, I recommend that you clip at least part of the reflection. Although the reflection is very impressive, it is not meant to be the centerpiece of the image and should be partially clipped to help center the focus of attention on the popcorn box.

Chapter 6

Photographic Restoration

One of the most powerful uses of Photoshop is for completing photographic restoration, but the restoration process can also be a frustrating experience. Unfortunately, photographic restoration is rarely a straightforward undertaking because of the uniqueness of individual circumstances as well as the large variety of physical defects that must typically be dealt with in a single image. In fact, it is common to see individual photographs that exhibit dust, scratches, lack of contrast, fading, local blurriness, stains, rips, and many more unique defects that essentially amount to a loss of image information.

It never ceases to amaze me how widely varied these defects can be, but I've also been pleasantly surprised on many occasions by the effectiveness of Photoshop in dealing with images that, at first glance, looked to be completely beyond repair. The fact is that you can restore images even when the damage is quite substantial. Keep in mind, however, that there are no prescribed techniques that work in all situations, so you must be flexible. In other words, you must be willing to experiment and modify your approach as you move along, based on the specific circumstances of the image you are working with. The good news is that there are usually multiple approaches that can be implemented for any given circumstance.

When using Photoshop to perform photographic restorations, it's important to implement an organized approach. In fact, I typically start with a duplicate image, and then I write down all the operations and individual settings that I implement as I proceed to edit the image. I also save all of the pre-feathered selections that I define along the way as well. Then once I complete the image, I edit the selections so that they're completely accurate and consistent before I implement a second edit with the same operations on another duplicate of the image. This approach provides me with the opportunity to work out the details on the first image before I proceed to complete the final image.

Exploring, Inspecting, and Preparing the File for Editing

Before we implement any local editing operations with the sample image of this chapter, we must first complete a few preparatory steps. In fact, we'll start by exploring the file that contains an additional layer as well as several channels. Once we know what's there, we'll then convert the image to grayscale before we inspect the image in detail to determine what editing is required to complete the final image.

I Open the file named GIRL.PSD and then choose View➡Fit on Screen. This file contains the scanned image of the antique photograph that we'll be restoring. The file also contains several items that will help us to quickly complete the technique.

In the Layers palette, the original image resides on the Background layer, which is accompanied by an additional layer named Hair. This layer is the final result that I produced after implementing the steps in the section named Advanced Hair Restoration. These steps may require some practice and are tedious as well as time consuming to complete properly. If you want, feel free to use the Hair layer in lieu of these steps to complete the technique quickly, but this layer should also remain invisible for now.

In the Channels palette, notice the 11 extra channels that are provided in addition to the RGB color channels. These channels contain predefined selections that we'll use as we move through the various editing operations of this chapter. These selections are predefined for your convenience so that you can quickly complete the operations of this chapter in the shortest time possible. Whenever these selections are called for, the text also explains how they were created so that you can create selections of your own if you want. It's not recommended, however, that you define your own selections, because the predefined selections are edited to be accurate and consistent throughout. In fact, we'll explore some of the operations that I implemented to define and edit these selections before providing them to you.

Now that we're familiar with the contents of the file, we'll move along to covert the image to grayscale in the next step. Once we've completed this operation, we'll then apply the Auto Levels command to draw out the image detail before we inspect the image.

By converting to grayscale, we preserve all the detail of the original, RGB-formatted image, but we no longer have to worry about matching color while performing editing operations. This is especially important in circumstances where an area is to be restored by sampling another part of the image. With the color information removed, we can readily use any part of the image that has the same texture and relative brightness to complete the operation.

2 Choose Image➡Mode➡Grayscale and then choose Don't Flatten when prompted. The sepia tone of the image has now been removed, but this will be reintroduced later in the chapter when the image has been fully restored.

3 Choose Image➡Adjust➡Auto Levels. This increases the contrast dramatically, but it also makes many of the inherent defects of the image more noticeable. Now use the Zoom tool to zoom in the view and examine the image more closely. Make note of the various defects that you see.

While inspecting the image, I immediately noticed several things that needed to be corrected. They included multiple occurrences of dust and scratches throughout the image; lack of contrast in the girl's face, hair, and especially in the pupil of the right eye; a stain along the left edge of the image; and the wearing away of the emulsion in several places, including the girl's forehead and the lower right side of her face. I also noticed some blurriness in the curly hair to the right of the face. As we move along, these items will all be corrected. In some cases, similar problems will be dealt with in different ways, and we'll begin by restoring the face.

Restoring the Facial Skin

As we proceed to complete the remaining operations of this technique, we'll start with the facial area and move progressively outwards. This chapter, however, will actually be broken down into sections based on the kinds of operations and tools that we use as we proceed. In this section, we'll edit the face to remove unwanted image detail using the Dust and Scratches filter, and I'm sure you'll be pleased with the results. In fact, the Dust and Scratches filter is often the tool of choice for removing unwanted detail, but it must be used carefully.

1 Using the Zoom tool, zoom in on the view so that the face fills the image window without being clipped and then load the selection from Channel #2. Choose Select➡Feather (Radius: 2.0 pixels). Now use the Clipboard to copy the contents of the selection to a new layer (Layer 1) and then rename the new layer Face. With the Face layer now active, turn on the Preserve Transparency option in the top, left corner of the Layers palette.

In this case, the selection in Channel #2 was originally defined with the Polygon Lasso tool to isolate the face, and we will feather it to preserve the natural transition of the face on Layer 1 to the surrounding pixels once it has been edited in the next several steps. By turning on the Layer Transparency option, we also ensure that the transparent regions of the layer will remain unaffected as operations are implemented.

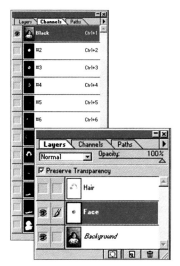

2 Load the selection from Channel #3. This selection was created with the Polygon Lasso tool to isolate the nondescript areas of the face. Choose Select➦Feather (Radius: 2 pixels). Now choose Filter➦Noise➦Dust and Scratches (Radius: 4 pixels, Threshold: 9 Levels) and then deselect the selection.

At this point, you'll still see quite a bit of blotchiness that the Dust and Scratches filter did not correct. Normally, I would not recommend the use of a Blur filter to remove this, since any applied blurring also removes texture that needs to be preserved, but the damage is quite significant and covers a large area of the face. As a result, it would take quite a long time to reconstruct the damaged areas by sampling pixels from other regions using the Rubber Stamp tool.

In this case, it turns out that the existing texture can easily be recreated artificially using a few commonly used filters. It's important to note that this approach must still rely on the existing image to provide the correct graduation in the overall brightness of pixels from one region to the next. Therefore, we'll work off the existing pixels by first applying a blurring filter to even out the blotchiness. Then we'll proceed to apply the additional filters that are required to generate the texture. The areas that we'll reconstruct include the entire right hand side of the face, the forehead, the chin, and surrounding pixels.

3 Load the selection from Channel #4. This selection was created using the Polygon Lasso tool to isolate the blotchy regions that we'll now begin to correct. Choose Select➡Feather (Radius: 1 pixel) and then choose Filter➡Blur➡Gaussian Blur (Radius: 4.5 pixels). Now deselect the selection. At this point, the blotchiness is mostly gone, but the right cheek could stand some extra blurring to even things out a bit more, and we'll do this in the next step.

There's no question that the Dust and Scratches filter is an effective tool for removing undesired defects from the image. The filter, however, must be used with care, since it can also reduce much wanted detail if applied improperly. In this case, the selection was defined to exclude the eyes, nostrils, and mouth to avoid this circumstance. By removing these elements, it was also acceptable to apply the filter with a greater strength than would have otherwise been possible. Nevertheless, the removal of these image elements does not totally free you to apply the filter at any strength, because even the nondescript areas of the face exhibit quite a bit of texture that you should strive to leave intact. This texture is necessary to help make the image look properly focused.

4 Load the selection from Channel #5. This selection was also created using the Polygon Lasso tool to isolate the region where we'll now apply the additional blurring. Choose Filter➡Blur➡ Gaussian Blur (Radius: 2.5 pixels). Deselect the selection. In the next step, we'll apply several filter operations to reintroduce a texture that matches the existing texture on the left side of the face.

In this case, the use of the Noise filter is a fairly obvious choice, and it works quite well, but I didn't know this until it was actually applied. In fact, I actually had to iterate through a couple of trial applications to develop the combination of filters and settings that we just used. In this case, you aren't required to implement any experimentation of your own, but this is something that you'll have to do when working with your own images. Nevertheless, the good news is that you'll spend a lot less time experimenting with filters once you've gained more experience with them.

5 Once again, load the selection from Channel #4 and choose Select➡Feather (Radius: 1.0 pixels). Now choose Filter➡Noise➡ Add Noise (Amount: 15, Distribution: Uniform, Monochromatic: Checked) and then choose Filter➡Blur➡Gaussian Blur (Radius: 0.4 pixels). Once again, choose Filter➡Noise➡Add Noise (Amount: 4, Distribution: Uniform, Monochromatic: Checked) and then deselect the selection. As you can see, the artificially created texture closely matches the original texture on the left cheek.

6 The face now looks much better, but it still looks a little bit overexposed and would look better with some added contrast. Choose Image➡Adjust➡Levels (Input Levels: 0, 0.80, 232). Now merge down the Face layer with the Background layer. At this point, the face looks much better. In fact, the added contrast makes it easier to distinguish the individual features, but there's still more to be done. For example, the pupils need some slight modifications as well, and we'll implement the necessary operations in the next step.

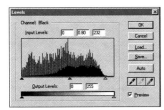

Improving the Appearance of the Eyes

Now that we've improved the appearance of the facial skin, problems with the eyes have become more readily apparent. More specifically, the pupil of the right eye needs to be darkened and both eyes need to be blurred to remove unwanted pixelation.

1 Using the Elliptical Marquee tool and/or the Polygon Lasso tool, select the pupil of the right eye. Choose Select➡Feather (Radius: 2 pixels) and then choose Image➡Adjust➡ Brightness/Contrast (Brightness: -25, Contrast: 0). Now choose Filter➡Blur➡Gaussian Blur (Radius: 0.3 pixels) and then deselect the selection.

2 Once again, use the Elliptical Marquee tool and/or the Polygon Lasso tool to select the left pupil. In this case, the pupil is already dark enough, but we're going to blur it a little to remove some of the pixelation so that it has a more glasslike appearance. Choose Select➡Feather (Radius: 2 pixels). Now press (Command+F) [Control+F] to reapply the Gaussian Blur filter with the same setting used on the right pupil and then deselect the selection. The face is now complete!

Exploring the Predefined Selections in Depth

Now that we've had a chance to work with many of the selections that were provided in the working file, it's probably a good idea to explore these selections in more detail. By doing this, I anticipate that you'll gain a better knowledge of the operations that were used to define them, an appreciation for their less obvious attributes, and a more thorough understanding of how the remaining selections can be used more effectively as we complete the final image. In fact, we'll begin by studying one of the selections in detail.

Before we load the selection, it's important to note that all of the predefined selections were edited to ensure that they accurately isolate the proper regions without overlap. In other words, all of the selections were edited to be completely consistent. To see these attributes more clearly, load the selection from Channel #12 and then use the Zoom tool to zoom in on the view over the girl's left shoulder. Notice how accurately the selection border follows the edge of the clothing. When implementing photographic restorations, it's important to define your selections accurately in order to ensure that your efforts result in the highest quality image possible. Now deselect the selection.

A good way to define accurate selections is to start with a rough selection that isolates the region of interest before zooming in on the view to edit local areas in more detail. Photoshop provides Add, Subtract, and Intersection capabilities that can be implemented with keyboard shortcuts to help you quickly complete local editing operations. But take your time and be resourceful!

For example, it is extremely common when implementing restorations to stumble across areas that lack contrast or appear blurred. It is often difficult in these situations to determine exactly where the selection border should be placed. In these cases, make a duplicate of the image and then change the Layer Apply mode of the duplicate layer to Multiply. This often increases the contrast of the image enough so that you can better judge the correct placement of the selection border.

Another good approach is to invert the pixels of the duplicate layer and then change the Layer Apply mode to Difference. As you can see in the accompanying image, this can be very effective. If necessary, adjust the layer opacity of the duplicate as well. There are numerous other combinations that you can use, and it doesn't hurt to do a little experimentation. Keep in mind that the duplicate layer can easily be discarded once it is no longer required.

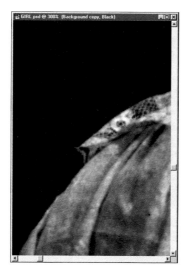

Another important characteristic of the predefined selections is that they are completely consistent. To see this more clearly, make Channel #2 active and then load the selection Channel #8. Notice that the common borders of the mask and the selection are completely consistent.

A good practice to follow when implementing photographic restorations is to save selections as you define them and before feathering is applied. In this case, the mask represents the selection that was used to isolate the face in Step 4. I defined this selection accurately and then immediately saved it to a new channel.

At a later point, I needed a selection to isolate the hair. Once again, I created an accurate selection, but this time I only defined the outside borders of the hair and then used the selection in Channel #2 to subtract out the region of the face. I then saved the newly defined selection immediately. In other words, this organized approach resulted in selections that were consistent and allowed me to leverage my previous work to ultimately save time.

Once the image was complete, I evaluated the image and modified my approach before implementing a second attempt to complete the restoration with a fresh copy of the image. Before moving on, make the RGB channel active and deselect the selection.

Basic Hair Restoration

Now that we've completed the face, we can start restoring the hair. In fact, we'll begin with some simple operations to clean up dust particles before we attempt to improve the appearance of the entire, under-saturated region of pixels near the hair ribbon. As you'll soon see, however, the operations of this section only have marginal effects on the appearance. Therefore, we'll quickly move on to the next section where we'll explore some more advanced techniques.

By turning on the Sample Merged option, we can use the Rubber Stamp tool to sample pixels from the Background layer while Layer 1 is active. When sampling pixels, be careful to make sure that the resulting texture is consistent and use the Eraser tool to eliminate mistakes. In the next step, we'll eliminate the region of under-saturated pixels next to the hair ribbon.

1 Create a new layer (Layer 1) and then select the Rubber Stamp tool from the toolbox. In the Rubber Stamp Options palette, reset the tool and then turn on the Sample Merged option. Now use the Rubber Stamp tool to sample neighboring pixels to eliminate small defects such as the dust particles previously mentioned. You may also target small defects by using the Eyedropper tool in conjunction with the Paintbrush tool and a small brush. Once you're finished and satisfied with the result, merge down Layer 1 with the Background layer.

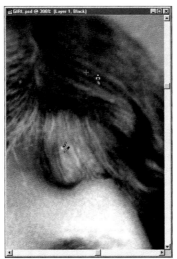

2 Load the selection from Channel #6. I created this selection using the Magic Wand tool with a tolerance of 4 by sampling the image just to the right of the ribbon to isolate the under-saturated pixels of that region. Choose Select➡Modify➡Expand (4 pixels). This eliminates the voids, but it also extends the region so that it overlaps the ribbon. To correct this, choose Select➡Modify➡ Contract (2 pixels). Now choose Select➡Feather (Radius: 2.0 pixels). In the next step, we'll use this selection to isolate our editing operations to the local region of under-saturated pixels.

Unfortunately, much of the hair outside the selection border exhibits little or no detail. As a result, you'll create noticeable repetitiveness if you sample pixels from the few areas where detail is present. This overall lack of detail will be dealt with in the next section where we'll actually paint in new strands of hair. At this point, your goal should be to sample other areas without trying to duplicate significant detail. Instead, concentrate on just matching the overall brightness and contrast of surrounding regions.

3 Create a new layer (Layer 1). Using the Rubber Stamp tool with the Sample Merged option still turned on, make corrections to the image by sampling pixels from the surrounding areas of the selection. When you're finished and satisfied with the result, deselect the selection and then merge down Layer 1 with the Background layer.

4 Create a new layer (Layer 1) and then load the selection from Channel #7. Now choose Select➡Feather (Radius: 2.0 pixels). Using the Rubber Stamp tool with the Sample Merged option still turned on, paint new pixels inside the selection by sampling adjacent pixels from surrounding areas in the backdrop and don't forget the portion of the selection above the hair ribbon. Once you're finished, deselect the selection and then refrain from performing any more editing operations to the region.

In this case, the selection is defined so that we can reduce the amount of apparent bushiness of the hair by sampling pixels from the surrounding backdrop. It's important to note that further editing operations are not required after deselecting the selection because any apparent mismatches will automatically be eliminated in a future step when we edit the backdrop for the entire image.

Advanced Hair Restoration

Unfortunately the operations of the previous section had only marginal effects on the appearance of the hair. Therefore, we'll have to take a more advanced approach. In this section, we'll add detail back into the image by painting individual strands of hair with the Paintbrush tool, but that's not all. We'll also add highlights and shadows to create the illusion of larger structures such as curls and waves within the hair as well.

Before proceeding, it's important to note that the ensuing steps will rely heavily on your artistic skills to implement. They can also be tedious and time consuming to properly complete. If you want to save time and move on after making an initial attempt to complete these steps, you may do so at any time. All that is required is that you delete any layers that you create in the ensuing text before you make the Hair layer visible, and then go directly to Step 8 of this section.

1 Load the selection Channel #8 and then choose Select➥Feather (Radius: 2 pixels). This selection will prevent you from affecting pixels outside the selected area and should remain active until you have finished Steps 1 through 7. Switch to the default colors and then switch the foreground and background colors. Select the Paintbrush tool from the toolbox. In the Brushes palette, choose the New Brush command from the palette pullout menu and then adjust the settings to (Diameter: 1 pixel, Hardness: 0%, Spacing 25%) to produce a very small brush. The new brush will now be selected in the Brushes palette. Make a note of its location because you may need to reselect it later. Now use the Zoom tool to zoom in the view so that the curly hair on the right-hand side of the face is enlarged as much as possible without being clipped.

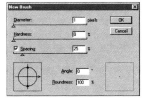
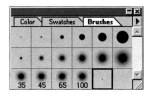

2 Create a new layer named White Strands. This is the first of three layers that you'll be using to add detail into the hair. Adjust the Layer opacity to 10%. Start painting individual strands over the blurred areas by stroking the Paintbrush in directions that are consistent with the apparent direction of the hair. This is a good start, but the white strands need to be balanced with black strands as well. Therefore, we'll now move on without painting hair for the entire head to add black strands to a new layer over the same exact region that we just painted the white strands.

3 Create a new layer named Black Strands and then adjust the Layer opacity to 40%. Switch the foreground and background colors. Now paint in additional strands over the same areas. This creates more detail that is really effective at reducing the apparent blurriness of the local area. The hair, however, still has a flat appearance and needs some highlights and shadows.

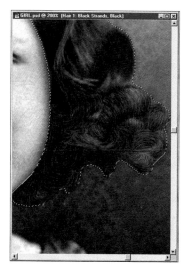

4 In the Brushes palette, select the New Brush command from the palette pullout menu and adjust the settings to (Diameter: 9 pixels, Hardness: 0%, Spacing: 25%). The new brush will now be selected in the Brushes palette. Make a note of its location because you may need to reselect it later.

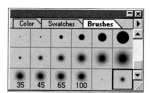

5 Create a new layer named Highlights and then adjust the layer opacity to 10%. Switch the foreground and background colors. Now use the Paintbrush tool to paint in highlights along the top edges of the individual curls. Also, use the Eraser tool to get rid of any mistakes that you make as you paint. These highlights now need to be softened. Choose Filter➥Blur➥Gaussian Blur (Radius: 2.0 pixels).

6 Create a new layer named Shadows and then adjust the layer opacity to **40%**. Switch the foreground and background colors. Now use the Paintbrush tool with the same brush to paint in shadows on the insides and along the bottom edges of the individual curls. As with the highlights, the newly painted shadows need to be softened. Choose Filter➡Blur➡Gaussian Blur (Radius: 1.5 pixels).

Now link the White Strands, Black Strands, Highlights, and Shadows layers and then merge the linked layers. Rename the resulting layer to Hair 1.

7 At this point, continue on to create additional hair strands, highlights, and shadows for the rest of the hair. Don't tackle everything at once. As you move along, select small regions and complete them using the same organized approach and layer naming convention presented in the previous six steps. Make sure to work with any detail that already exists. Once you are done, deselect the selection.

At this point, the Layers palette may contain several layers named Hair, Hair 1, Hair 2, Hair 3, and so on. If you want, create additional layers to paint strands along the edges of the hair that stick out from the region now that the Channel #8 selection is no longer active. Also, delete the Hair layer if you do not intend to use it with this image. Now link all the layers except the Background layer and then merge the linked layers. Rename the resulting layer to Hair.

8 Make the Background layer active. Once again, load the selection Channel #8 and then choose Select➠Feather (Radius: 2.0 pixels). Now use the selection to copy the contents of the selection on the Background layer to a new layer (Layer 1). With Layer 1 now active, change the layer apply mode to Multiply and then adjust the layer opacity to 35%. Now choose Layer➠Flatten Image. At this point, the hair is complete. Let's move on to make corrections to the neck and forearm.

Restoring the Neck and Forearm

1 Duplicate the Background layer to create a new layer named Background copy. Load the selection from Channel #9. Choose Select➠Feather (Radius: 2 pixels) and then choose Filter➠Dust and Scratches (Radius: 6 pixels, Threshold: 6 Levels). Now choose Filter➠Noise➠Add Noise (Amount : 5, Distribution: Uniform, Monochromatic: Checked) and then deselect the selection. The texture on the neck now looks much better, but the jawline is not very distinct. We'll correct this with the Gradient tool.

2 Switch to the default colors and then select the Gradient tool. In the Gradient Tool Options palette, reset the tool and select Cancel when prompted. Specify Foreground to Transparent in the Gradient field. Now drag out a gradient from pixel location (500,750) to (500,800) and then deselect the selection. Merge down the Background copy layer with the Background layer. The neck is done. Now let's move on to make corrections to the forearm.

3 Duplicate the Background layer to create a new layer named Background copy. Load the selection from Channel #10. Choose Select➡Contract (2 pixels) and then choose Select➡Feather (Radius: 1 pixel). Now Select the Rubber Stamp tool from the toolbox. In the Rubber Stamp Options palette, reset the tool. Now use the Rubber Stamp tool to eliminate the under-saturated pixels near the elbow by sampling other pixels from surrounding areas on the forearm.

4 Choose Filter➥Blur➥Gaussian Blur (Radius: 3.0 pixels). This reduces the blotchiness. Now the arm needs to have texture added back in. Choose Filter➥Noise➥Add Noise (Amount: 5, Distribution: Uniform, Monochromatic: Checked). Deselect the selection. The forearm is now complete except for one detail. The forearm does not blend properly with the backdrop. This will be dealt with as you make corrections to the backdrop in the next section. Before proceeding, merge down the Background copy layer with the Background layer.

Editing the Backdrop

Now that we've edited the girl, the backdrop is the only part of the image that still needs to be edited. In this case, we'll essentially blur the image using the Dust and Scratches filter to produce a very smooth looking, abstract pattern for the background, but first we'll define a composite selection to limit the application of the filter to the region of the backdrop. We'll also define this selection to have a heavily feathered border along the bottom edge of the forearm so that the forearm blends seamlessly into the backdrop. In fact, we'll concentrate on building this characteristic into the selection first.

1 Load the selection from Channel #11 and then choose Select➥Feather (Radius: 10 pixels). This isolates the area that we want to have blended, which is what the large feathering radius will accomplish. We will now combine this selection with a selection that isolates the backdrop. Once combined, the resulting selection will automatically create the blending effect while the backdrop is edited. Save the selection to a new channel (Channel #13) and then deselect the selection.

2 Load the selection from Channel #12 and then invert the selection. Now hold the (Command+Shift) [Control+Shift] keys and load the selection from Channel #13 to intersect it with the current selection. With the Background layer currently active, use the resulting selection to copy the backdrop to a new layer and name it Backdrop. With the Backdrop layer now active, turn on the Preserve Transparency option in the Layers palette. We are now ready to edit the backdrop to create a more pleasing appearance. In this case, we'll use the Dust and Scratches filter to even things out, but before we do that, we must first eliminate large eyesores that the Dust and Scratches filter won't be able to eliminate completely on its own.

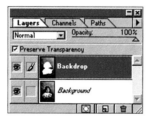

3 Using the Rubber Stamp tool, eliminate the dark stain along the left edge of the image by sampling neighboring pixels. Don't worry about blending the resampled area. The Dust and Scratches filter will do that for you when it is applied in the next step.

4 Choose Filter➡Noise➡Dust and Scratches (Radius: 16 pixels, Threshold: 0 Levels). This smoothes out the backdrop quite nicely. Let's now add some texture back in. Choose Filter➡Noise➡Add Noise (Amount: 20, Distribution: Uniform, Monochromatic: Checked) and then choose Filter➡Blur➡Gaussian Blur (Radius: 2.0 pixels). The image looks great!

At this point, all retouching operations are complete. Now is a good time to save the grayscale image before proceeding to implement any further operations. It's also a good idea to save the file to a format that also saves all the channels of the file as well. In this case, I saved the file as GIRL_30.PSD and you'll find this file on the CD-ROM.

Final Image Presentation

At this point, there are several options that you have for presenting the image in a more final form. The operations of this section will show you how you can add a sepia tone back into the image and then apply the concepts of Chapter 4 to vignette the image as well. Another excellent option is to colorize the image and frame it. Otherwise, continue to follow the remaining operations of this technique.

1 Before we can reintroduce the original tone, we must first convert back to the RGB color mode. Choose Image➡Mode➡RGB color and then select Flatten when prompted. Now choose Image➡Adjust➡Color Balance (Levels: 55, 30, -10, Midtones). That's it! The original sepia tone has been restored and now we'll move on to produce a vignette for the image as well.

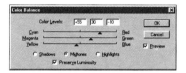

2 Create a new layer named Paper, set the foreground color to off-white (R: 240 G: 230 B: 210), and then fill the layer with the foreground color. Choose Filter➡Noise➡Add Noise (Amount: 30, Distribution: Gaussian, Monochromatic: Checked) and then choose Filter➡Blur➡Gaussian Blur (Radius: 2.0 pixels). Now choose Filter➡Blur➡Motion Blur (Angle: 45 degrees, Distance: 40 pixels). This creates a pleasing background with slight color variations upon which we'll now place a vignetted version of the image.

3 Duplicate the Background layer. With the duplicate layer (Background copy) now active, rename the active layer to Layer 1. Now move Layer 1 to the top of the stack in the Layers palette. In this case, the vignetting will be produced by preparing a mask that will then be applied as a layer mask to Layer 1. Once the layer mask has been applied, we can then center the image within the vignette borders defined by the mask. Let's begin.

4 Select the Elliptical Marquee tool and place the cursor at pixel location (50,100). Now drag out a selection with a width and height of 900 × 1250. Choose Select➡Feather (Radius: 15 pixels) and then save the selection to a new channel (Channel #16). Make Channel #16 active. The feathered selection now appears as a mask in the image window. Deselect the selection.

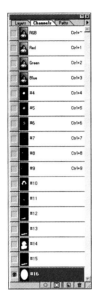

5 Select the Magic Wand tool. In the Magic Wand Options palette, reset the tool and specify a value of 4 in the Tolerance field. Now define a new selection by sampling the center of the solid white region of the mask and choose Select➡Feather (Radius: 15 pixels). Now invert the selection. Hold the (Command+Option+Shift)[Control+Alt+Shift] keys and click Channel #16 in the Channels palette. This creates a new selection that isolates the border of the mask by intersecting the current selection with the Channel #16 mask.

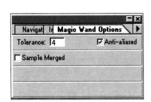

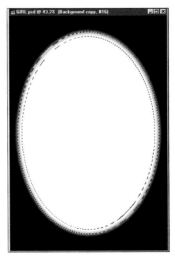

Because the active selection and the mask both had feathered edges before the intersection operation was performed, there is a smooth transition of the noise to both the white interior and black exterior regions of the mask. We are now ready to apply the mask.

6 We'll now use this selection to edit the Channel #16 mask by adding some noise around the edges of the ellipse. Choose Filter➡Noise➡Add Noise (Amount: 200, Distribution: Uniform, Monochromatic: Checked). Now deselect the selection.

7 Load the selection from Channel #16 and then make the RGB channel active. With Layer 1 and the Channel #16 selection both active, choose Layer➡Add Layer Mask➡Reveal Selection. In the Layers palette, unlink the layer mask and then click the thumbnail image that appears on Layer 1. With Layer 1 still active, use the Move tool to move the image of the girl down and to the left in the image window.

Now choose Layers➡Flatten Image. The image is now complete!

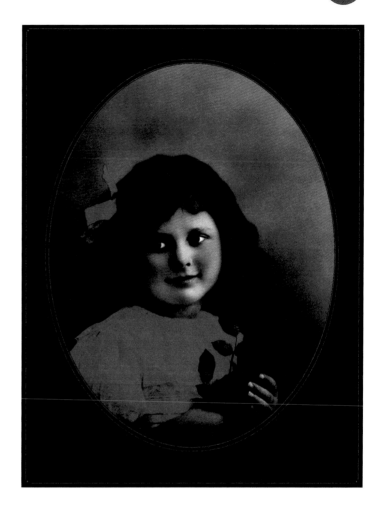

Chapter 7

Changing the Weather: Simulating Rain and Snow

Sometimes the operations that are required to produce a specific effect are not as straightforward as we'd all like. In fact, the simulation of falling rain and snow is a excellent example of an effect that typically requires a lot of experimentation to develop a set of suitable operations and related settings that work well to produce a natural and pleasing result. The simulation of adverse weather conditions, however, involves much more than just simulating the falling precipitation. In fact, this technique could easily be characterized as a composite technique because it borrows several operations from other techniques previously presented.

For example, we'll end up borrowing concepts from Chapter 11, "Working with a Central Theme," to change the apparent time of day. We'll also borrow concepts from Chapter 2, "Simulating Water Reflection," to introduce a water-based reflection over the roadway surface in the foreground so that it appears to look wet.

The two forms of falling precipitation (both rain and snow) will also have to be introduced in such a manner that they exhibit a property known as atmospheric perspective. Atmospheric perspective is characterized by different qualities in different settings. In the presence of falling rain and snow, however, it's often characterized by the obscuration of distant objects (by the falling precipitation) more than objects in the foreground.

As such, atmospheric perspective is a depth cue that the human brain uses to interpret the relative position of objects in the environment, and it can be used by artists for the same purpose. In our case, atmospheric perspective will be incorporated because of the presence of prominent objects in both the foreground and background of the final image that we'll be producing. Therefore, we'll have to follow a slightly more complicated approach when we introduce the textures for simulating the falling precipitation.

Preparing the Source Image

In the next several steps we'll implement modifications that will correct the appearance of the source image to improve its color contrast and reduce the brightness of surfaces that are strongly illuminated.

1 Open the file named BUILDING.TIF. Let's take a few moments to become familiar with the contents of this file. In the Layers palette, the source image resides on the Background layer, which is accompanied by another layer named Automobile. This layer contains the same automobile that was used in the sample image of Chapter 7 and I've pasted it into this file using the same concepts presented in that chapter. At the moment, the layer is invisible and should remain so for the time being. I've also provided you with two alpha channels as well as two paths. These items are provided for your convenience so that we can quickly move through some of the more complicated steps of the technique. Nevertheless, you will be required to create additional selections, channels, and masks as we proceed. Needless to say, there's a lot that needs to be done so let's get started!

Before moving on, take a few moments to assess the quality of the image. Notice that the brick surface of the roadway has a washed out appearance which needs to be corrected. Also, the protruding wall that resides directly behind the street lamp has a much brighter appearance than the other walls of the building.

This brightness is a result of its direct exposure to the strong light of the sun during midday. The final weather conditions that we'll be introducing, however, are characterized by a lighting environment that is more ambient in nature. Therefore, we'll have to darken the protruding wall so that it more closely matches the brightness of the other walls of the building. We'll also have to darken the entire image since the overall lighting environment is much brighter than what we would normally expect to see during a snow storm or even a downpour.

2 Load the selection from Channel #4. This selection was created using the Polygon Lasso tool and was defined to isolate the lower portion of the image right up to the edge of the dark shadows located directly in front of the bushes while excluding the base of the street lamp. Choose Select➡Feather (Radius: 2 pixels). Now choose Image➡Adjust➡Brightness/Contrast (Brightness: -50, Contrast: +30) and then deselect the selection.

At this point, we've improved the appearance of the roadway, let's move on to make adjustments to the protruding wall.

3 Open the Paths palette and then make Path 1 active. This is a closed path that I defined using the Pen tool to isolate the bright areas of the wall's brick surface. Choose the Make Selection command from the Paths palette pullout menu and specify a feathering radius of 1 pixel in the dialog box that appears. Now that we have the selection, we no longer need the path. Select the Turn Off Path command from the palette pullout menu as well.

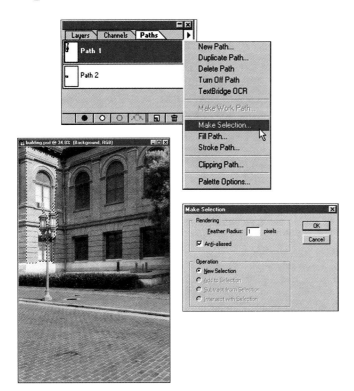

4 With the selection still active, use the clipboard to copy the contents of the selection to a new layer (Layer 1) and then change the layer apply mode to Multiply.

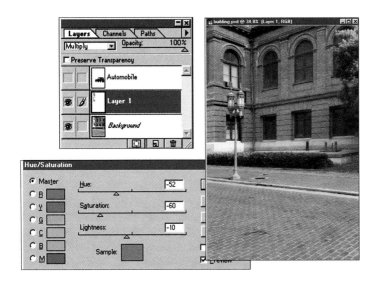

It's important to note that a lot of experimentation was required to obtain a path that accurately isolated the bright regions of the brick surface. In fact, the paths capability was used instead of the Polygon Lasso tool so that I could more easily implement an iterative approach in defining the final selection that we used. In other words, I assessed the appearance of the image after completing the operations of this step and then refined the path so that I could re-implement the step to obtain a better quality result. This may seem to be a very labor intensive task and it is, but the fact of the matter is that it took much less time to iterate through the refinements than it took to define the initial path.

At this point, the overall brightness of the protruding wall's brick surface matches the brightness of the other walls even though it displays a slightly higher contrast. Notice that the shadowed regions of the protruding wall are darker than comparable regions on the other walls. This difference is perfectly acceptable and it is not necessary to make any additional modifications to produce high quality results in the final images. In fact, extensive editing of the selection would be required to achieve marginal improvements. Nevertheless, you'll find a fully edited selection saved as Channel #5, which you may use if you wish.

To use the Channel #5 selection, delete Layer 1 and then load the selection from Channel #5. With the Background layer active, now implement the operations of this step once again. The selection in Channel #5 was used to produce the sample images that are displayed with this chapter to achieve a slightly better appearance.

Before proceeding, merge down Layer 1 with the Background layer and delete Channel #5. It is no longer needed. Now let's move on to complete the concrete base of the wall.

5 In the Paths palette, make Path 2 active. Choose the Make Selection command from the Paths palette pullout menu. Specify a feathering radius of 1 pixel in the dialog box that appears and then choose the Turn Off Path command from the palette pullout menu as well. Now use the Clipboard to copy the contents of the selection to a new layer (Layer 1).

6 With Layer 1 active, choose Image➥Adjust➥Desaturate and then choose Image➥Adjust➥Brightness/Contrast (Brightness: -28, Contrast: +50). Now choose Image➥Adjust➥ Hue/Saturation. Turn on the Colorize option and then adjust the slider controls to (Hue: 30, Saturation: 8, Lightness: 0). I determined these settings by experimentation and the result looks quite good, but we've also produced some unwanted edge effects that need to be eliminated.

7 Select the Rubber Stamp tool. In the Rubber Stamp Options palette, reset the tool and then turn on the Sample Merged option. Now select a medium sized, soft brush from the Brushes palette. With Layer 1 still active, use the Rubber Stamp tool to clean up any offending edge effects. Once you are done and pleased with the result, merge down Layer 1 with the Background layer.

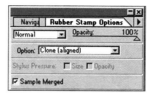
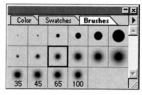

By using an adjustment layer, we maintain more control over the appearance of the image because we can alter the settings of the adjustment layer at any time as we proceed. The Image Dimmer layer will eventually have to be merged down with the background image to simplify some of the operations that we'll be implementing later on. We'll also have to edit the adjustment layer before then. Therefore, its best to leave it in place for the time being.

In addition to the local adjustments that we've already completed, we also need to reduce the overall brightness of the image to a level that is more appropriate to the weather conditions that we'll be introducing. In this case, we'll actually darken the image enough to change the apparent time of day.

8 Choose the New Adjustment Layer command from the Layers palette pullout menu. In the dialog box that now appears, name the layer Image Dimmer and then specify Hue/Saturation as the Type. In the Hue/Saturation dialog box that next appears, adjust the settings to (Hue: 0, Saturation: 0, Lightness: -80).

9 At this point, make the Automobile layer active. This image was prepared from a grayscale, antique photograph, which was also used to complete the sample image of Chapter 7 as well. For more information on the actual operations that were used to prepare the image, refer to that chapter, which also describes how to composite the image with a working image as well. In this case, I supplemented the compositing operations presented in Chapter 7 with a skewing operation to alter the apparent perspective of the automobile so that it now matches the perspective of the background image.

Adding in Artificial Light

In many of the previous steps of this technique, we implemented several operations to remove the harshness of the original lighting environment. We also applied an adjustment layer that darkened the entire image to change the apparent time of day. Now we'll move along to add light back into the image to create a lighted environment that is dominated by an ambient component with the street lamp as the primary source.

In this case, we'll follow an approach that initially borrows some of the concepts of Chapter 16 to make the street lamp appear to be self-luminated. We'll then move on to implement several additional adjustments to the surfaces of objects in the vicinity of the lamp so that the final lighting scheme looks more natural and consistent.

1 Create a new layer named Lamp Light. Set the foreground color to yellow (R: 245 G: 225 B: 25) and zoom in the view so that the top of the street lamp dominates the image window. Select the Line tool from the toolbox. In the Line Tool Options palette, reset the tool and then specify a Line Width of 8 pixels. Now draw lines over the glass windows of the lamp as shown.

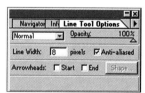

2 Choose Filter➡Blur➡Gaussian Blur (Radius: 9.0 pixels). Now duplicate the Lamp Light layer. With the duplicate layer active, choose Filter➡Blur➡Gaussian Blur (Radius: 20 pixels) and then merge down the duplicate layer with the Lamp Light layer.

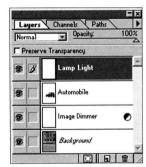

The glowing effect looks very realistic, but additional modifications must be made to the image so that the scene appears to have a consistent lighting scheme. More specifically, we'll have to lessen the effect of the Image Dimmer layer over the foreground surfaces. This must be done such that the apparent brightness of these surfaces appears to fall off as a function of distance from the lamp. Actually, things are a bit more complicated since the automobile image resides above the Image Dimmer layer in the Layers palette. As a result, the surfaces of the automobile need to be darkened instead. It may seem tempting to move the automobile image below the Image Dimmer layer, but this actually complicates future operations and therefore, it's best to edit the Automobile layer separately.

In addition to making brightness alterations, we'll also have to shift the color of foreground surfaces towards the yellow color of the apparent illuminating source (the street lamp). These modifications will be made to all foreground surfaces that appear to be directly illuminated. In fact, the modifications will be implemented by applying the color so that it falls off as a function of distance in the same way as the brightness.

The good news is that we can easily and quickly complete the involved operations with the help of two new selections that we'll define and save before implementing any of the modifications. In this case, the first selection will be defined to isolate the driver's side of the automobile, and the second selection will be defined as a gradient mask to attenuate future selections as a function of distance from the illuminating source.

It's important to note that the back vertical edge of the automo-bile is curved so that we should expect to see a gradual transi-tion in the lighting from the driver's side to the back side of the automobile. Therefore, the selection that isolates this region must be defined so that its right, vertical border is feathered by a large amount to provide this gradual transition automatically whenever the selection is used.

3 Using the Rectangular Marquee tool, define an oversized selec-tion that isolates the driver's side of the automobile as shown. I defined the selection from pixel location (170,740) to (880,1400).

When defining your own selection, it's important that the selec-tion's right, vertical border reside directly above the back, vertical edge of the automobile. If you have defined the selection correct-ly, this edge of the selection should just barely graze the left edge of the automobile's license plate. Also, the remaining three bor-ders of the selection should clear the automobile by at least 20 pixels on all other sides.

4 With the rectangular selection still active, choose Select➡Feather (Radius: 16 pixels). Hold the (Command+Option+Shift)[Control+Alt+Shift] keys and then load the layer transparency selection from the Automobile layer to intersect it with the current selection.

At this point, save the selection to a new channel (Channel #5) and then deselect the selection. We'll now move on to create the second selection.

5 In the Channels palette, create a new channel (Channel #6). Switch to the default colors and then switch the foreground and background colors. Make the RGB channel visible so that the image window now displays the mask and the image simultaneously.

Select the Gradient tool from the toolbox. In the Gradient Tool Options palette, reset the tool and then choose Cancel when prompted. With Channel #6 still active, drag out a gradient from pixel location (225,585) to (1185,1785).

At this point, the selection appears to be isolating the entire image except the front end of the automobile. In actuality, all of the pixels of the automobile are selected, but the pixels near the front of the automobile appear outside the selection border because they are less than 50% selected. We'll now use this selection to darken the surfaces of the automobile.

As a result of the way we defined the selection, the backside of the automobile was darkened more than the driver's side. The backside was also darkened to the same brightness as the pixels in the surrounding environment, while the driver's side was darkened

The two selections are now complete, and we can now move on to edit the image. Make the RGB channel active and make Channel #6 invisible. We'll begin by altering the surfaces of the automobile.

6 Load the selection from Channel #5. Hold the (Command+Option+Shift)[Control+Alt+Shift] keys and load the selection from Channel #6 to intersect it with the current selection. Now invert the selection.

7 Make the Automobile layer active. Now choose Image➡ Adjust➡Hue/Saturation (Hue: 0, Saturation: 0, Lightness: -80) to darken the contents of the selection. Do not deselect the selection when you are done. Remember, these are the same settings we used with the Image Dimmer layer.

continues

continued

from the distance of the light source of the street lamp. We'll now use the selection to add in the yellow hue of the illuminating source.

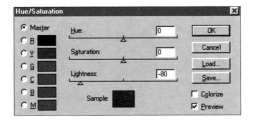

8 With the foreground color still set to yellow (R: 245 G: 225 B: 25), create a new layer (Layer 1). Now invert the selection and then choose Select➟Modify➟Contract (4 pixels). Fill the selection with the foreground color and then deselect the selection. Now change the layer apply mode to Multiply and then merge down Layer 1 with the Automobile layer.

In this case, the selection was contracted to avoid unwanted edge effects that would have otherwise occurred. I determined the radius of contraction by way of experimentation. Let's now move on to adjust the brick surfaces of the roadway and sidewalk.

This new selection will be used in lieu of Channel #6 for the same purpose. Because Channel #7 differs from Channel #6 only in its brightness, Channel #7 selects pixels less strongly than Channel #6 and sometimes produces a more natural result when used with a particular operation. We'll use Channel #7 instead of Channel #6 in this step as well as a few other upcoming steps.

9 In the Channels palette, duplicate Channel #6. With the duplicate channel (Channel #7) now active, choose Image→Adjust→Brightness/Contrast (Brightness: -70, Contrast: 0).

10 Now make the RGB channel active once again. Load the selection from Channel #4 and then choose Select→Feather (Radius: 2.0 pixels). Hold the (Command+Option+Shift) [Control+Alt+Shift] keys and load the selection from Channel #7 to intersect it with the current selection. The resulting selection now appears to be isolating a small region along the left edge of the image.

In actuality, all of the pixels in the foreground are selected, but most of them are less than 50% selected so that they appear outside the selection border that Photoshop displays. Let's now use this selection to edit the Image Dimmer layer.

11 Make the Image Dimmer layer active. Before proceeding, it's important to note that all adjustment layers work with masks. In the Channels palette, notice that the corresponding mask of the Image Dimmer layer is active while the RGB channel is visible. Make the Image Dimmer Mask channel visible as well.

At this point, the image window is actually displaying the mask of the Image Dimmer layer over the image with the selection borders of the selection that we created in the previous step, but the mask of the Image Dimmer layer is completely clear so that only the image and the selection borders are seen. Now we'll use the selection to edit the mask.

12 Switch to the default colors and then fill the selection with the foreground color. Deselect the selection and then make the Image Dimmer Mask channel invisible once again. Notice that the brick surface of the roadway and the sidewalk have a brighter appearance that diminishes as a function of distance from the base of the street lamp. In the Layers palette, merge down the Image Dimmer layer with the Background layer. Let's now move on to add in the yellow hue to the surfaces that we just brightened.

13 Load the selection from Channel #4 and then choose Select➥Feather (Radius: 2.0 pixels). Hold the (Command+Option+Shift)[Control+Alt+Shift] keys and then load the selection from Channel #6 to intersect it with the current selection. Now create a new layer (Layer 1). With the foreground color still set to yellow (R: 245 G: 225 B: 25), fill the selection with the foreground color and then deselect the selection. Change the layer apply mode to Multiply and then merge down Layer 1 with the Background layer.

14 With the Background layer active, create a new layer (Layer 1). Select the Line tool from the toolbox. In the Line Tool Options Palette, reset the tool and then specify a Line Width of 35 pixels. Switch to the default colors and then draw a line from pixel location (360,1224) to (1154,1304) and then another from (360,1224) to (868,1306). Now draw one more line from pixel location (860,1306) to (1154,1304) and then choose Filter➡ Blur➡Gaussian Blur (Radius: 20 pixels). Merge down Layer 1 with the Background layer.

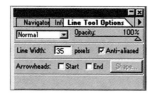

Simulating Wet Surfaces

Here's where we really get into the core operations of changing the weather. In order to produce a final result that looks realistic, it's not enough to simply introduce a texture that simulates the falling precipitation. In fact, we must implement further modifications to the foreground surfaces so that they look wet. Because wet surfaces produce strong reflections, this is the predominant characteristic that we'll rely upon to create the effect. Actually, we only need to alter the surface of the roadway and the side-walk which makes the task a bit easier to complete.

1 Make the Automobile layer invisible. Now load the selection from Channel #4 and use the Polygon Lasso tool to edit the selection so that it isolates only the surface of the roadway and the sidewalk. In other words, hold the (Option)[Alt] key and then use the Polygon Lasso tool to subtract from the selection. Now choose Select➡Feather (Radius: 2.0 pixels) and then save the selection to a new channel (Channel #8). Deselect the selection.

2 Make the Automobile layer visible once again. Duplicate the Background layer and then rename the duplicate layer (Background copy) to Water Reflection. Now choose Layer➡Transform➡Flip Vertical and then choose Layer➡Transform➡Numeric. In the dialog box that now appears, specify a relative pixel position of (0,300). Make sure that the scaling values for the width and height fields are both set to 100%. Load the selection from Channel #8 and then invert the selection. Now press Delete to clear the portions of the Water Reflection that do not fall over the roadway and sidewalk surfaces. Deselect the selection and then delete channel #8 since it is no longer required.

3 Now duplicate the Automobile layer. Choose Layer➡ Transform➡Flip Vertical and then choose Layer➡Transform➡ Numeric. In the dialog box that now appears, specify a relative pixel position of (0,475). Choose Layer➡Transform➡Skew and then move the center handle on the left edge of the transformation tool upwards until the Info palette displays a parallelogram value of 7.0 degrees. Don't apply the transformation just yet.

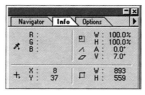

4 Now move the center handle along the bottom edge of the transformation tool to the left until the Info palette displays the settings as shown.

In this case, it's important to note that the angles used with the Transformation tool were chosen to match the reflected image to the existing perspective of the automobile. They were also chosen to provide a more close match-up of the tires in the reflected image to the tires of the actual automobile. When placing a reflection, it's desirable to place the reflection so that it matches the original object as closely as possible at the base of the object.

5 Link the Water Reflection layer to the active layer and then make the Water reflection layer active. Merge the linked layers and then choose Filter➡Blur➡Gaussian Blur (Radius: 5.0 pixels). At this point, we've already gotten a good start with the reflection, but there are a few modifications that still need to be implemented to increase its realism. In order to make the necessary modification, we'll first need to define one additional selection.

6 Create a new channel (Channel #8). Switch to the default colors and then fill the channel with the foreground color. Choose Filter➡Noise➡Add Noise (Amount: 999, Distribution: Gaussian, Monochromatic: Checked) and then choose Filter➡Blur➡Motion Blur (Angle: 0 degrees, Distance: 100 pixels). Now choose Image➡Adjust➡Brightness/Contrast (Brightness: -90, Contrast: +70). We'll now use this selection to modify the reflection.

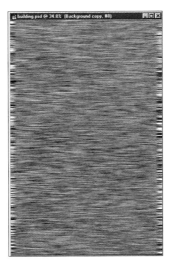

7 Load the selection from Channel #7. Hold the Shift key and then load the selection from Channel #8 to add it to the current selection.

With the Reflection layer still active, press Delete and then deselect the selection. Now delete Channel #8 since it is no longer required.

The strength of the reflection now varies as a function of distance from the base of the street lamp. It also exhibits local strength variations that look very natural. These local variations were made possible with the use of the channel mask that we created in the previous step. Although the reflection looks very realistic, its overall appearance looks a bit weak and needs to be strengthened.

8 Duplicate the Water Reflection layer and then choose Filter➡Blur➡Gaussian Blur (Radius: 10.0 pixels). Now adjust the layer opacity of the duplicate layer to 50%. Before proceeding, link the Water Reflection layer with the duplicate layer. Now make the Water Reflection layer active and then merge the linked layers.

The reflection looks excellent! In fact, we've actually produced our first variant weather condition. Even though we have not yet introduced any falling precipitation, the current image is consistent with the way we would expect the scene to look just after a rainfall has occurred. We're now ready to introduce textures to simulate the falling precipitation. Let's now move on to add in textures that simulate falling precipitation.

Creating the Falling Precipitation

At this point, our goal is to produce two separate images that exhibit the variant weather conditions of falling rain and falling snow. In order to produce these images, we'll introduce textures that simulate falling precipitation in such a manner that they also have the characteristic of atmospheric perspective. We'll start by first producing the image that simulates falling snow because it is the easier of the two conditions to produce.

1 With the Water Reflection layer still active, create a new layer named Snow 1. Switch to the default colors and then switch the foreground and background colors. Now fill the layer with the foreground color and then choose Filter➡Noise➡Add Noise (Amount: 50, Distribution: Gaussian, Monochromatic: Checked). Change the layer apply mode to Hard Light and then adjust the layer opacity to 10%.

This is just one of two layers that are required to complete the final effect, but before we create the second layer, we need to modify this layer to produce the effect of atmospheric perspective in the final result. This will require that we first define an additional selection as a channel mask.

2 Create a new channel (Channel #8). Select the Gradient tool from the toolbox. In the Gradient Tool Options palette, reset the tool and then select Cancel when prompted. Now switch to the default colors and then drag out a gradient from the bottom center to the top center of the image window.

Make the RGB channel active and load the selection from Channel #8. With the Snow 1 layer still active, press Delete to reduce the apparent density of the falling snow in the foreground. Deselect the selection.

Before we move on to simulate falling rain, let's make a few more modifications to the existing image so that you can see how easy it is to produce a whole spectrum of images in which the severity of the apparent weather condition is varied.

3 Make the Automobile layer active and then create a new layer named Snow 2. Now set the foreground color to medium gray (R: 125 G: 125 B: 125) and then fill the layer with the foreground color. Choose Filter➡Noise➡Add Noise (Amount: 50, Distribution: Gaussian, Monochromatic: Checked). Now change the layer apply mode to Hard Light and then adjust the layer opacity to 25%.

4 Make the Water Reflection layer active and then load the layer transparency selection from the layer as well.

Now create a new layer named Accumulated Snow. Switch to the default colors and then switch the foreground and background colors. Now fill the selection with the foreground color and then deselect the selection. Choose Filter➡Blur➡Gaussian Blur (Radius: 5.0 pixels) and then adjust the layer opacity to 40%. Now make the Snow 2 layer active and then adjust the layer opacity to 60%. Also, make the Water Reflection layer invisible.

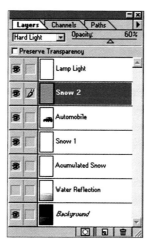

As you can see, there are a lot of refinements that can be implemented to adjust the image to your own particular tastes. Let's now move on to create falling rain. Before proceeding, make the Snow 1, Snow 2, and Accumulated Snow layers invisible and then make the Water Reflection layer visible once again.

In order to create a realistic texture to simulate the falling rain, we'll have to apply no less than six filters. Therefore, the task is divided among the next two steps. Once we have the basic texture, we'll then perform one additional operation to account for atmospheric perspective in the final image.

5 Make the Water Reflection layer active and create a new layer named Rain 1. Set the foreground color to medium gray (R: 125 G: 125 B: 125) once again, and then fill the layer with the foreground color. Choose Filter➡Noise➡Add Noise (Amount: 100, Distribution: Gaussian, Monochromatic: Checked) and then choose Filter➥Blur➥Motion Blur (Angle: 80, Distance: 100). Now choose Filter➥Artistic➥Plastic Wrap (Highlight Strength: 20, Detail: 14, Smoothness: 4). Change the layer apply mode to Hard Light and then adjust the layer opacity to 20%. We're halfway there.

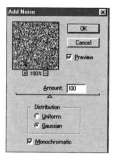

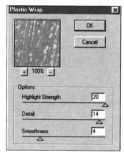

6 Choose Filter➥Other➥High Pass (Radius: 5.0 pixels) and then choose Filter➥Blur➥Gaussian Blur (Radius: 1.0 pixel). Finally, choose Filter➥Blur➥Motion Blur (Angle: 80 degrees, Distance: 10 pixels).

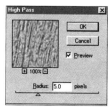

At this point the texture actually looks quite good, but we have one more operation to complete.

7 Duplicate the Rain 1 layer and then rename the duplicate to Rain 2. Move the Rain 2 layer above the Automobile layer in the Layers palette. With the Rain 2 layer active, load the selection from Channel #8 and then press Delete to help simulate atmospheric perspective.

If you wish, adjust the layer opacities of the Rain 1 and Rain 2 layers to alter the intensity of the falling rain and the level of atmospheric perspective.

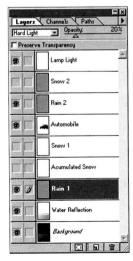

Chapter 8

Using Light to Set the Mood

Light is such an integral part of the physical world in which we live that we often take it for granted. In a functional sense, light is what allows us to perceive the world around us, but light is much more than that. Light is also a transient phenomenon that exhibits an infinite variety of form which varies with the time of day, the weather, and various other conditions of the environment.

Nevertheless, the characteristics of light and its interaction with the environment are predictable. In fact, the human brain has adapted to assign significance to its various qualities that can be manipulated to control the essence and mood of a particular setting. Consider for a moment the difference in mood that can be created by changing the light of a setting from the strong, white, directional light of midday to the soft, yellow, ambient light that is often produced by candles after dark. While the first condition often evokes no emotional response at all, the latter condition can create a sense of comfort, well being, and tranquillity.

The good news is that you can often use Photoshop to alter the apparent lighting of a scene to create these qualities where they don't already exist, and that is exactly what we'll do in this chapter by altering the apparent lighting of a very simple table setting. As with most of the techniques in this book, we'll start with an ordinary photograph that we'll edit to improve the composition before we introduce the final lighting condition. As you'll soon see, the change in the lighting helps to further enhance the thoughts of remembrance and eternity that the composition already evokes with the inclusion of the lit candles, the antique photographs, and the wall hanging that displays a winding road through the autumn leaves.

Removing the Unwanted Perspective

In this section, we'll improve the composition of the image in which we'll change the apparent time of day. In this case, the image displays an interior setting containing several candles and two photographic frames that are sitting on a glass tabletop.

In order to produce a more interesting and natural appearance in the image, the camera was positioned slightly higher than the glass surface of the table when the photograph was taken. This provides a natural viewing angle because most table top surfaces are viewed from above in common experience. The chosen viewing angle also creates a more visually interesting image because it enables us to see the glass reflections of objects sitting on the surface as well.

There is, however, one obvious downside to this vantage point, which happens to be the existing vertical perspective that makes the candles all appear to be leaning inward. Nevertheless, this undesirable characteristic can be edited out of the image, and this is exactly what we'll do in this section.

I Open the file named CANDLES.PSD. You'll notice that the background layer contains the basic image, but the file also contains an extra layer named Candles that resides directly above the Background layer and is currently not visible. We'll make use of the Candles layer in this section and its purpose will be explained shortly, but the layer should remain invisible until it is needed. In the next step, we'll begin by copying the candles to a new layer where we can edit them independently of the other objects in the scene.

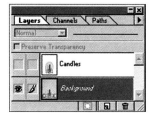

2 Load the selection from Channel #4. Now choose Select➡ Feather (Radius: 6.0 pixels) and then use the clipboard to copy the contents of the selection to a new layer (Layer 1). In this case, I defined the selection with the Polygon Lasso tool.

3 If the Info palette is not currently visible, choose Window➡ Show Info. With Layer 1 now active, choose Layer➡Transform➡ Perspective. Now move the upper right handle of the Transformation tool outward until the Info palette displays an angle of -2.5 degrees and then apply the transformation. This is already a major improvement, but the candles still appear to be leaning slightly to the left, and we'll want to correct this as well.

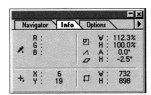

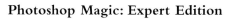

4 Choose Layer➡Transform➡Skew. Now move the top center handle of the Transformation tool to the right until the Info Palette displays an angle of -0.3 degrees and then apply the transformation.

The candles now look great, but the back edge of the table no longer has a continuous appearance. In this case, it's tempting to move the transformed region upward to re-establish a continuous appearance for the edge. Doing so, however, would cause misalignments between the bases of the candle holders and their corresponding reflections in the glass. Therefore, we'll have to implement another transformation to scale the height of the image on Layer 1 upward until the back edge is properly aligned.

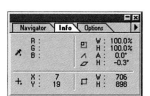

5 Choose Layer➡Transform➡Scale. Now move the top center handle of the Transformation tool upward until the Info Palette displays a vertical scaling value of 110.0%, and then apply the transformation.

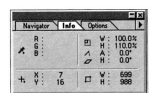

Softening the Shadows

At this point, we've completed all the necessary transformations to remove the unwanted perspective, such that the candles still appear to be seamlessly integrated with the rest of the image. Now we'll move on to soften the existing shadows that the candle holders cast on the back wall. In order to complete the ensuing steps, we'll make extensive use of a pre-saved path that I defined using the Pen tool to trace out the contours of the candles in the transformed image. You'll find this path saved as PATH 1 in the Paths palette.

If you implemented all of the previous transformations exactly as instructed, you should be able to use this path with the transformed image that you created on Layer 1. We'll play it safe, however, and use the transformed image on the Candles layer instead. This is the image that I produced, which is also the image that I worked with when defining the PATH 1.

1 Delete Layer 1 and then make the Candles layer active. In the Paths palette, make PATH 1 active and then choose the Make Selection command from the Paths palette pullout menu. In the dialog box that now appears, specify a feathering radius of 0.5 pixels. Now choose the Turn Off Path command from the pullout menu as well.

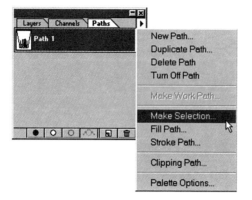

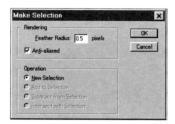

2 Choose Image➡Adjust➡Brightness/Contrast (Brightness: +17, Contrast: -60) and then choose Image➡Adjust➡Hue/Saturation. When the dialog box appears, turn on the Colorize option and then adjust the settings to (Hue: +55, Saturation: +12, Lightness: -1). Now deselect the selection so that you can better inspect the results.

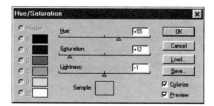

In this case, the Brightness/Contrast settings were chosen to soften the shadows, but they also reduced the overall color saturation of the region that the Hue/Saturation controls were used to reintroduce. As a result of these operations, we've effectively softened the shadows of the candle holders without creating significant mismatches in the overall color and brightness of the region with its surroundings. Nevertheless, there is still a very slight mismatch that we'll want to eliminate, and we'll do this in the next step.

At this point, the Candles layer is complete, but before we can merge this layer with the Background layer, there's one last shadow that we need to modify—the shadow cast by the picture frame on the right hand side of the image.

3 With the Candles layer still active, load the layer transparency selection from the layer as well. Choose Select➡Modify➡Border (16 pixels) and then choose Select➡Modify➡Expand (16 pixels). Select the Rectangular Marquee tool from the toolbox. Hold the (Option)[Alt] key and drag out a selection from pixel location (200,1160) to (1000,1550). Now choose Filter➡Blur➡Gaussian Blur (Radius: 12.0 pixels) and then deselect the selection.

4 With the Rectangular Marquee tool still selected, drag out a selection from pixel location (850,1200) to (1020,1500). Now choose Select➡Feather (Radius: 16 pixels). In the Paths palette, make PATH 1 active and then select the Make Selection command from the palette pullout menu. In the dialog box that now appears, specify a feathering radius of 0.5 pixels and then turn on the Intersect with Selection option. Now select the Turn Off Path command from the pullout menu as well. At this point, we now have a selection that isolates the local region of the shadow, which we'll soften using the same controls that we used previously.

5 Make the Background layer active. Now choose Image➡Adjust➡Brightness/Contrast (Brightness: +9, Contrast: -60) and then choose Image➡Adjust➡Hue/Saturation. When the dialog box appears, turn on the Colorize option and then adjust the settings to (Hue: +55, Saturation: +9, Lightness: -1). Deselect the selection and then choose Layer➡Flatten Image.

Compositing in the Additional Elements

Now that we've completed the Background image, it's time to move on to introduce some additional elements that increase the visual interest of the image as well as complete the basic composition. In this case, we'll start by introducing a framed image as a wall hanging behind the candles and vase. I'm sure you've noticed by now that there are two empty picture frames that need filling as well, and we'll fill them too with completed images from other techniques of this book. Finally, we'll also introduce flames to the candles to make them appear to be lit.

As you'll soon see, these additional elements really improve the appearance of the image, which will be enhanced even further in the next section when we implement the core operations of this technique to change the apparent time of day. Let's get started by introducing the wall hanging.

1 Open the file named AUTUMN.TIF. This is the image that we'll use for the wall hanging, but before we copy it to the working image, we'll add a frame to create a more natural appearance. Using the Rectangular Marquee tool, define a selection from pixel location (20,20) to (747,1003) and then invert the selection. Switch to the default colors and then set the foreground color to burgundy (R: 100 G: 50 B: 50). Fill the selection with the foreground color. Switch the foreground and background colors and then choose Edit➡Stroke (Width: 2 pixels, Location: Center, Opacity: 100%). Deselect the selection. This frame enhances the image quite nicely and we'll now move on to integrate the image as a wall hanging in the working image.

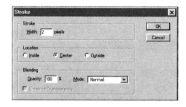

2 Choose Select➡All and then choose Edit➡Copy to copy the image to the clipboard. Save and close the AUTUMN.TIF file. Now that we're back in the working file, choose Edit➡Paste to place the image on a new layer and then rename the layer to Wall Photo. Now choose Layer➡Transform➡Numeric and specify the settings as shown.

As you can see, the image is properly centered and sized, although it certainly doesn't appear to be hanging on the wall behind the candle holders

continues

continued

as we wish. In order to create this effect, we'll make use of a layer mask to limit the display of the composited image. First, we'll implement a few more operations to create a layer drop shadow that will help to anchor the composited image into its surroundings.

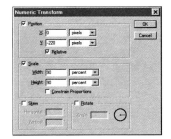

3 Now make the Background layer active and then create a new layer (**Layer 1**). Load the layer transparency selection from the **Wall Photo** layer. Switch to the default colors and then fill the selection with the foreground color. Deselect the selection. Now choose Layer➡Transform➡Numeric and specify a relative pixel position of (5,5). Turn off all other input fields before applying. Choose Filter➡Blur➡Gaussian Blur (Radius: **6.0** pixels) and then adjust the layer opacity to **80%**. Make the Wall Photo layer active. Link Layer 1 to the Wall Photo layer and then merge the linked layers. We'll now move on to create a layer mask so that the image appears to be hanging on the wall behind the candles.

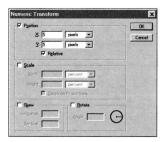

4 In the Paths palette, make PATH 1 active. Choose the Make Selection command from the palette pullout menu. In the dialog box that now appears, specify a feathering radius of 0.5 pixels. Now choose the Turn Off Path command from the pullout menu as well. With the Wall Photo layer still active, choose Select➡Modify➡Expand (1 pixel) and then choose Layer➡Add Layer Mask➡Reveal Selection. Before proceeding, choose Layer➡Flatten Image.

In this case, the selection is expanded to avoid unwanted edge effects that would have otherwise occurred. It's important to note that the selection remains feathered. The wall hanging now looks to be properly integrated with its surroundings. Now we'll move on to composite in some photographs into the empty frames. We'll start by introducing a photograph into the left frame.

5 Open the file named PHOTO1.TIF. Choose Select➡All and then choose Edit➡Copy to copy the image to the clipboard. Close the image without saving. Now that we're back in the working file, choose Edit➡Paste to place the image onto a new layer and then rename the layer to Photo1. Choose Layer➡ Transform➡Numeric and specify the settings as shown.

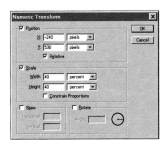

Now we'll distort the image into the frame. Before you begin, zoom in on the view so that you can implement this operation more accurately. Now choose Layer➡Transform➡Distort and then match the corner handles of the Transformation tool to the inside corners of the picture frame so that the image appears to reside in the frame. Finally, choose Image➡Adjust➡ Brightness/Contrast (Brightness: -30, Contrast: 0).

At this point, the photograph looks great! However, some additional operations need to be implemented because we must also modify the reflection of the picture frame as well.

6 Duplicate the Photo 1 layer. With the duplicate layer (Photo 1 copy) now active, choose Layer➧Transform➧Flip Vertical and then use the Move tool to move the reflected photograph to match its upper-left corner to the upper-left inside corner of the picture frame reflection as shown and apply the transformation.

Now choose Layer➧Transform➧Skew and then move the right center handle of the Transformation tool until the reflected photo is properly matched to the reflection of the frame and apply the transformation.

7 Using the Rectangular Marquee tool, define a selection from pixel location (60,1567) to (220,1599) and then press Delete to trim the photo from extending beyond the top surface of the glass. Deselect the selection. Now choose Filter➡Blur➡Gaussian Blur (Radius: 1.0 pixels) and then adjust the layer opacity to 50%.

8 Now repeat the operations of Steps 5–7 to introduce an image into the right picture frame using the file named PHOTO2.TIF. Once the second image has been introduced, choose Layer➡Flatten Image. In the next step, we'll introduce the candle flames to complete the basic composition of the image.

9 Open the file named FLAME.PSD. In the Paths palette, make the FLAME PATH active and then choose the Make Selection command from the palette pullout menu. In the dialog box that now appears, specify a feathering radius of 0.5 pixels. Now choose the Turn Off Path command from the pullout menu as well and then choose Edit➡Copy to copy the flame to the clipboard. Close the file without saving. Now that you're back in the working file, choose Edit➡Paste to place the flame onto a new layer (Layer 1). Choose Layer➡Transform➡Scale and then use the handles of the Transformation tool to scale the flame and place it on any one of the four candles as shown.

10 Now introduce flames to the remaining candles by successively duplicating the active layer and then using the Move tool to move each duplicate flame image to the remaining candles. Once you are done, link all of the flame layers and then merge the linked layers. Rename the resulting layer to Flame.

Altering the Lighting Conditions

Up until now we've implemented a lot of operations that have substantially improved the composition of the original image. But this is where we really begin to get into the core operations of this technique. In the ensuing steps, we'll first darken the entire image before we implement additional operations to brighten local regions. More specifically, we'll brighten the entire lower third of the image so that the eye is drawn more immediately to the framed images on the tabletop. We'll also brighten the immediate regions around each candle flame as well as the tips of the candles to create the natural glow that we would expect to see. Once we've brightened these areas, we'll also add in a little bit of yellow color to create more warmth in the image as well, and I'm sure you'll like the effect.

This dims the image quite substantially in a uniform manner. In the next two steps, we'll begin to add light back in by first brightening the lower third portion of the image. Then we'll move on to concentrate on the local regions around the candle flames.

I Make the Background layer active and then create a new layer named Dimmer. With the Dimmer layer now active, switch to the default colors and then fill the layer with the foreground color. Now adjust the layer opacity to 70%.

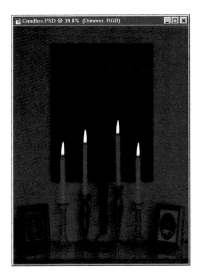

2 Using the Elliptical Marquee tool, define a selection from pixel location (0,200) to (1199,1199). Create a new channel (Channel #5). With Channel #5 now active, set the foreground color to dark gray (R: 110 G: 110 B: 110) and then fill the selection with the foreground color. Choose Layer➡Transform➡Numeric and specify a relative pixel position of (0,700). Make sure to turn off all other input fields before applying. Now choose Filter➡Blur➡Gaussian Blur (Radius: 100 pixels). In the next step, we'll load this channel as a selection which we'll use to lighten the lower third portion of the image.

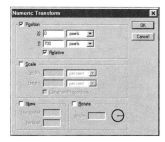

Remember, no selection borders are displayed for this selection so don't forget to deselect the selection once you're through with it.

3 Load the selection from Channel #5 and then choose OK when prompted. Because none of the pixels are more than 50% selected, no selection border will be displayed. Therefore, it's important that we not forget to turn off the selection once we're through with it. Make the RGB channel active. With the Dimmer layer still active, press Delete to lighten the lower third portion of the image and then deselect the selection. Now we'll move on to brighten the immediate regions around each of the four candles.

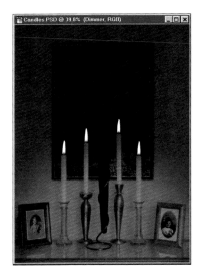

4 Using the Elliptical Marquee tool, define a selection from pixel location (650,620) to (780,800). Create a new channel (Channel #6). With Channel #6 now active, set the foreground color to gray (R: 140 G: 140 B: 140) and then fill the selection with the foreground color. Now choose Filter➡Blur➡Gaussian Blur (Radius: 30 pixels). In the next step, we'll load this channel as a selection which we'll use to lighten the image in the next step.

5 Load the selection from Channel #6 and then make the RGB channel active. With the Dimmer layer still active, press Delete to brighten the immediate region around the flame that is selected.

With the Elliptical Marquee tool still selected, place the cursor inside the circular shaped selection border and then drag the selection over the wick of one of the remaining three candles. Press Delete once again to brighten the local region around the flame. Now use the selection to complete the remaining two candles in the same manner. Once you've completed all four candles, deselect the selection. We'll now move on to create a glowing appearance on the tips of the candles.

6 In the Paths palette, make PATH 1 active and then choose the Make Selection command from the palette pullout menu. In the dialog box that now appears, specify a feathering radius of 0.5 pixels. Now choose the Turn Off Path command from the pullout menu as well and then choose Select➡Modify➡Expand (1 pixel). Invert the selection. Using the Polygon Lasso tool, hold the (Option+Shift)[Alt+Shift] keys and define a selection across the tips of the candles as shown.

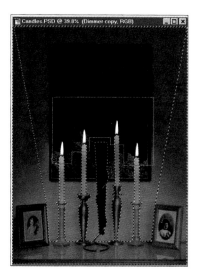

This will produce a final, composite selection that isolates the tips of the candles. With the Dimmer layer still active, press Delete to brighten the tips of the candles and then deselect the selection.

Even though the tips of the candles are bright, the appearance is not very natural and we'll have to implement a few more operations and therefore, we'll implement a few improvements. More specifically, we'll create another composite selection in much the same way that we did in this step. We'll then use the selection to blur the brightened candle tips so that there is a gradual falloff in brightness down the stems of the candles.

7 In the Paths palette, make PATH 1 active and then choose the Make Selection command from the palette pullout menu. In the dialog box that now appears, specify a feathering radius of 0.5 pixels. Now choose the Turn Off Path command from the pullout menu as well and then choose Select➡Modify➡Expand (1 pixel). Invert the selection. Using the Polygon Lasso tool, hold the (Option+Shift)[Alt+Shift] keys and define a selection across the base of each candle as shown.

This will produce a final, composite selection that isolates the entire stem of each of the four candles. Now choose Filter➡Blur➡Gaussian Blur (Radius: 20.0 pixels) and then deselect the selection. At this point, the effect already looks quite good, but the image has a very cold feel to it so we'll want to warm things up a bit.

8 With the Dimmer layer still active, create a new layer named Warmth. Now load the layer transparency selection from the Dimmer layer and then invert the selection. Set the foreground color to yellow (R: 250 G: 250 B: 100) and then fill the selection with the foreground color. Deselect the selection. Now change the layer apply mode to Overlay and then adjust the layer opacity to 80%. The image is now complete! Choose Layer➡Flatten Image.

Creating a Fantasy Image

It seems that new Photoshop users always seem to learn the basic capabilities of the application in the same order. At the beginning of the list are the Cut and Paste operations, which can probably be attributed to the fact that most of us have had plenty of practice with cutting and pasting ever since our first introduction to construction paper, scissors, and rubber cement. Even though Photoshop doesn't require rubber cement to paste images together, the basic operations are still the same.

Things, however, can get much more complicated in Photoshop with the use of layer masks, feathered selections, channels, and other powerful capabilities that enable us to perform these basic operations to achieve higher quality in the images that we produce. In fact, we'll make extensive use of these capabilities to produce the sample image of this technique, and the surprising thing is that the Cut and Paste operations (with all their Photoshop variations) are really all that is required to produce professional quality images even when your source images are not that remarkable. In fact, this technique is a prime example of how to combine multiple source images of average quality to produce an excellent final image.

Creating the Planet

1 Open the file named STARS.JPG. This file contains an image of a star field that will serve as the background over which the remaining elements of the montage will be introduced.

In this case, we'll create the planet Neptune from scratch. It turns out that Neptune is not that difficult to simulate because the real planet is basically a featureless, cyan-colored orb that exhibits only slight variations in color.

2 Create a new layer named Planet. Select the Elliptical Marquee tool from the toolbox and place the cursor at pixel location (200,200). Now hold the Shift key and drag out a selection with a final width and height of 800 × 800 pixels.

Now set the foreground color to cyan (R: 85 G: 155 B: 155) and then fill the selection with the foreground color. Choose Filter➡Noise➡Add Noise (Amount: 200, Distribution: Uniform, Monochromatic: Not Checked) and then choose Filter➡Blur➡Motion Blur (Angle: 30 degrees, Distance: 60 pixels).

In addition to the numerous Cut and Paste operations that we'll be completing as part of this technique, we'll also be using the Photoshop filters to paint a few of the elements of the final image as well. In fact, we'll start by creating an artificial version of the planet Neptune using some basic Photoshop filters to create a realistic result. Then we'll proceed to the ensuing sections where we'll introduce the surface of the water, the god Neptune himself, and finally the layer of clouds between the god and the planet.

In general, it's easier to introduce the background elements before the foreground subject, but this is not the best approach in this exercise because we need to know the exact location of the god before we can add the clouds. The reason for this is because we have to introduce two images to complete the final appearance of the clouds, which in turn, requires us to hide a seam behind the rising arm of the god. In order to do that, we need to know the exact location of the arm. Hence, the image of the god will have to be introduced first.

Now choose Filter➡Distort➡Glass (Distortion: 14, Smoothness: 13, Texture: Frosted) and then Choose Filter➡Blur➡Gaussian Blur (Radius: 5.0 pixels). With the selection still active, we'll now move on to some additional operations to complete the final appearance of the planet.

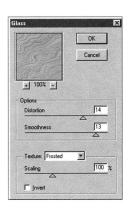 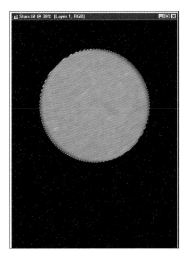

3 Select the Gradient tool from the toolbox. In the Gradient Tool Options palette, reset the tool and then choose Cancel when prompted. Now specify Foreground to Transparent in the Gradient field. Switch to the default colors and then drag out a gradient from pixel location (280,850) to (920,350). Choose Select➡Modify➡Contract (16 pixels) and then choose Select➡Feather (Radius: 2.0 pixels).

At this point the planet is complete and looks great. Let's now move on to complete the foreground elements of the image, which include the surface of the water and the image of Neptune.

Invert the selection and then press the Delete key to trim away the unwanted edge effects that were created by the Motion Blur filter in the previous step. Deselect the selection. Now choose Layer➡Transform➡Numeric and specify the settings as shown.

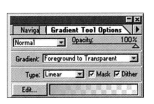 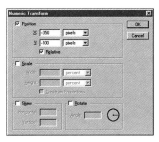

Compositing the Foreground Elements

There's no question that the god Neptune is the centerpiece of the final image. The image that we'll be using to represent him is derived from a photograph of a statue called "The Awakening," which is located in Washington, DC. Unfortunately, the photograph doesn't present the statue with the proper proportions that we desire for our final image, so we'll implement several operations to alter the appearance of the photo before compositing it into the working image.

The other foreground element that must be composited is the surface of the water from which Neptune appears to be rising. This can be easily completed in a single step, which we'll do now before moving on to complete the more involved operations of introducing the image of the god.

1 Open the file named WATER.JPG. Choose Select➡All and then use the clipboard to copy the contents of the selection to a new layer named Water Surface located above the Planet layer in the Layers palette. Now choose Layer➡Transform➡Numeric and specify the settings as shown. Load the layer transparency selection from the Water Surface layer and then choose Select➡Modify➡Border (16 pixels).

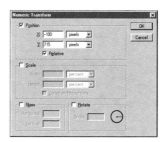

These last operations are implemented to create a more dream-like appearance by slightly exaggerating the color saturation of the image and blurring the horizon so that it isn't so sharply defined. In this case, we were able to isolate the horizon using the Borders command because the remaining borders of the water surface reside outside the frame of the image.

Now choose Select➡Modify➡Expand (4 pixels) and then choose Filter➡Blur➡Gaussian Blur (Radius: 5.0 pixels). Deselect the selection and then choose Image➡Adjust Hue/Saturation (Hue: 0, Saturation: 20, Lightness: -15). Now close the WATER.JPG file without saving it and let's move on to the main subject of our figure.

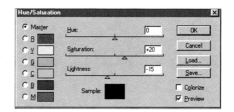

2 Open the file named STATUE.PSD. As already mentioned, we'll be implementing a few modifications to this image so that it better serves its purpose. More specifically, the arm will be enlarged with respect to the other two elements of the statue so that it takes on a more prominent appearance. We'll also need to skew the arm so that the statue's right hand becomes more prominent without creating an unnatural appearance.

In order to make better use of space in the final image, we'll also want to slightly reposition the three elements of the statue with respect to each other. As a result, we'll have to follow an approach in which we modify each element separately. To accomplish this, we'll have to copy each element out of the background, and I've provided three predefined paths that will allow us to quickly move along through the involved operations.

3 In the Paths palette, make the Hand path active and then choose the Make Selection command from the palette pullout menu. In the dialog box that now appears, specify a feathering radius to 1 pixel. Now select the Turn Off Path command from the palette pullout menu as well. With the selection still active, use the clipboard to copy the contents of the selection to a new layer just above the Background layer and then rename the layer to Hand.

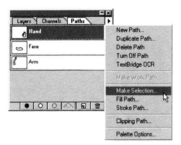

4 With the Hand layer now active, make the Background layer invisible and then use the Rectangular Marquee tool to define a selection from pixel location (1150,1030) to (1500,1150). Hold the (Command+Alt)[Control+Alt] key and load the layer transparency selection from the Hand layer to subtract it from the rectangular selection. Now choose Select➠Modify➠Expand (8 pixels) and then choose Select➠Feather (Radius: 8.0 pixels).

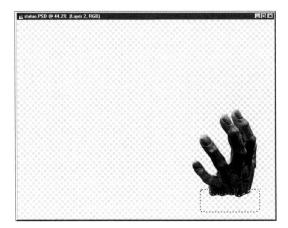

Press the Delete key to feather the bottom edge of the hand and then deselect the selection. Now choose Layer➞Transform➞ Numeric. In the dialog box that appears, specify the settings as shown.

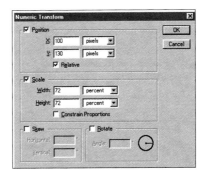

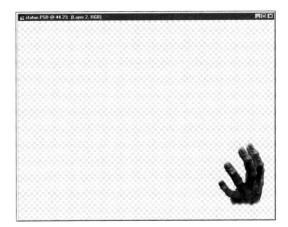

Before proceeding, make the Background layer active and then make the Hand layer invisible. We'll now move on to complete the face.

5 In the Paths palette, make the Face path active and then choose the Make Selection command from the palette pullout menu. In the dialog box that appears, specify a feathering radius of 1 pixel. Now select the Turn Off Path command also located in the palette pullout menu. With the selection still active, use the clipboard to copy the contents of the selection to a new layer just above the Background layer in the Layers palette, and then rename the layer to Face.

6 With the Face layer now active, make the Background layer invisible and then use the Rectangular Marquee tool to define a selection from pixel location (450,800) to (1200,900). Hold the (Command+Alt) [Control+Alt] key and load the layer transparency selection from the Face layer to subtract it from the rectangular selection. Now choose Select➥Expand (8 pixels) and then choose Select➥Feather (Radius: 8.0 pixels).

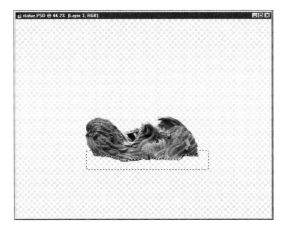

Press the Delete key to feather the bottom edge of the hand and then deselect the selection. Now choose Layer➥Transform➥ Numeric. In the dialog box that appears, specify the settings as shown.

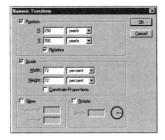

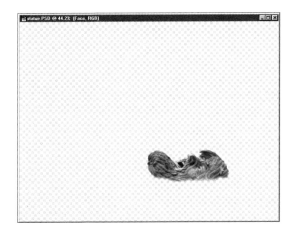

Before proceeding, make the Background layer active and then make the Face layer invisible. We'll now move on to complete the arm.

7 In the Paths palette, make the Arm path active and then choose the Make Selection command from the palette pullout menu. In the dialog box that appears, specify a feathering radius to 1 pixel. Now select the Turn Off Path command also located in the pull-out menu. With the selection still active, use the clipboard to copy the contents of the selection to a new layer just above the Background layer in the Layers palette and then rename the layer to Arm.

8 With the Arm layer now active, make the Background layer invisible and then use the Rectangular Marquee tool to define a selection from pixel location (150,760) to (400,850). Hold the (Command+Alt) [Control+Alt] key and then load the layer transparency selection from the Arm layer to subtract it from the rectangular selection. Now choose Select➡Expand (8 pixels) and then choose Select➡Feather (Radius: 8.0 pixels).

Press the Delete key to feather the bottom edge of the hand and then deselect the selection. Now choose Layer➡Transform➡ Numeric. In the dialog box that now appears, specify the settings as shown.

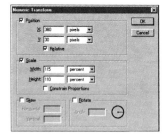

At this point, the arm looks much more prominent, but there's still one additional modification that needs to be made.

In the photo, the forearm looked small in comparison to its base, which made the hand appear more distant than what we desired. In the final image, we want the hand to appear as prominent as possible because it will be holding a planet. Therefore, we implemented the modification to increase the size of the hand as much as possible without creating an unnatural appearance.

9 Choose Layer➡Transform➡Perspective and then adjust the top-left handle of the transformation tool until the Info palette displays a Perspective angle of -5.0 degrees.

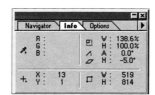

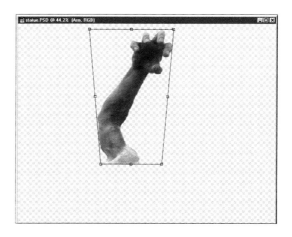

At this point, all of the body parts have been sized and positioned to their final states. We can now merge these elements to a single layer.

10 With the Arm layer still active, make both the Face and Hand layers visible. Now link the Face and Hand layers to the Arm layer.

Merge the linked layers and then choose Image➡Adjust➡ Hue/Saturation. In the dialog box that now appears, turn on the Colorize option and then adjust the slider controls to (Hue: 65, Saturation: 20, Lightness: -40). At this point, the appearance of the statue is complete and we're ready to copy it to the working image.

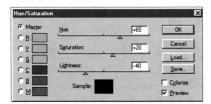

11 Select➡All and then use the clipboard to copy the contents of the selection back to the working image onto a new layer named Roman God. Now choose Layer➡Transform➡Numeric and specify the settings as shown to move Neptune to his final position above the surface of the water. Save the STATUE.PSD file if you wish, and then close the file as well. We'll now move on to introduce the orb into the hand of the god's rising arm.

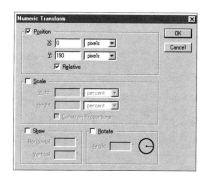

Introducing the Orb

In order to create the orb, we'll make a duplicate of the planet and scale it to fit in Neptune's hand. We also, however, want the orb to be encircled by the god's fingers as well, which requires a layer mask to hide the areas of the orb that overlap the fingertips wrapping around the orb. We'll start by creating the orb and then we'll move on to edit the appearance of the orb by developing the mask before applying it.

I Duplicate the Planet layer and name the new layer Orb. Now move the Orb layer so that it resides directly above the Roman God layer in the Layers palette. Choose Image➡Adjust➡ Hue/Saturation (Hue: -70, Saturation: 20, Lightness: -10) and then choose Layer➡Transform➡Numeric and specify the settings as shown. The orb should now appear to be hovering in front of the hand.

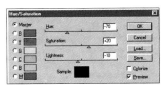

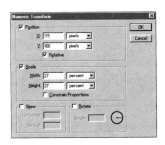

2 We'll now develop a layer mask to push the orb into the god's hand. With the Orb layer still active, adjust the layer opacity to 30% and then use the Zoom tool to zoom in on the view so that the semi-transparent orb and the underlying hand dominates the view of the image window.

Now use the Pen tool and the related Path Editing tools to define a smooth, closed path that traces out the outlines of the fingers as shown. When defining this path, it's important to flare out the path so that it extends outside the apparent borders of the orb as you move from one finger to the next. In the Paths palette, select the Save Path command from the palette pullout menu and accept the default settings to name it Path I. In the next step, we'll use this path to create a composite selection, which we'll then apply as a layer mask to the Orb layer so that it appears to be gripped by the hand.

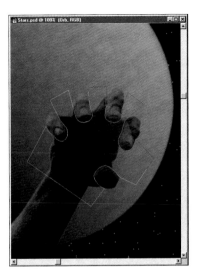

3 Adjust the layer opacity of the Orb layer back to 100%. Now choose the Make Selection command from the Paths palette pullout menu. In the dialog box that appears, specify a feathering radius of 1 pixel and then choose the Turn off Path command from the palette pullout menu as well. Now choose Layer➡Add Layer Mask➡Reveal Selection. At this point, the orb should appear to reside inside the grip of the hand, but there's one last modification that needs to be implemented.

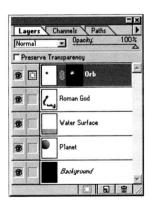

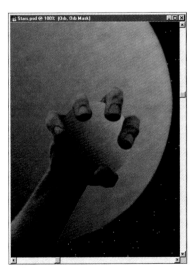

4 In the Paths palette, make Path I active. Once again, choose the Make Selection command from the palette pullout menu and then specify a feathering radius of I pixel. Invert the resulting selection. Now select the Turn Off Path command from the palette pullout menu as well. Create a new layer and name it Shadow. Switch to the default colors and then fill the selection with the foreground color. Deselect the selection. Now choose Filter➡Blur➡Gaussian Blur (Radius: 3.0 pixels) and then adjust the layer opacity to 80%. Now choose Layer➡Transform➡ Numeric and specify the settings as shown.

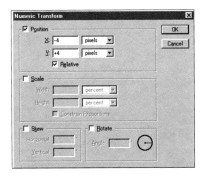

Grouping causes Photoshop to define a layer as a mask to limit the display of material on layers that reside above that layer in the Layers palette. In this case, the mask was defined from the Orb layer and applied to the Shadow layer. Notice that the thumbnail image on the Shadow layer is now indented to indicate that the grouping has occurred. Conversely, we could have loaded the layer transparency selection from the Orb layer and then applied the selection as a layer mask to the Shadow layer to achieve the same effect.

It's important to note that grouping is not the same as linking. In fact, they're completely different operations that have nothing to do with each other. Linking tells Photoshop to perform identical transformations on all linked layers whenever any one of the layers in the linked list is transformed. More specifically, when you move, scale, rotate, or skew a layer, all layers that are linked to that layer will be transformed in exactly the same way. Linking also has some other important attributes during layer merge operations as well. In fact, I encourage you to study the Photoshop user manual to become more familiar with their use.

5 Now choose the Layer Options command from the Layers palette pullout menu. In the dialog box that appears, turn on the Group with Previous Layer option.

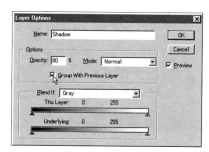

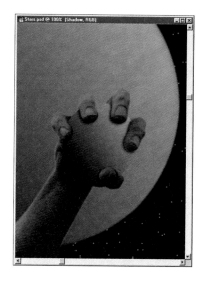

The drop shadow is complete and the orb blends seamlessly with its surroundings so that it appears to reside in the hand. Let's now move on to add in the clouds along the horizon of the water. Before proceeding, make the Planet layer active.

Compositing the Clouds

In this case, we'll be introducing the clouds from two separate photographs. These images were chosen because they just so happen to present a visually interesting composition when combined that fits nicely with the composition of the working image.

I Open the file named CLOUDS1.JPG. Choose Select➡All and then use the clipboard to copy the image to a new layer just above the Planet layer in the working file. Rename the layer Clouds and then close the CLOUDS.JPG file. Now choose Layer➡Transform➡Numeric and specify the settings as shown. Let's now add the second image.

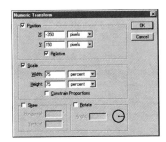

Open the file named CLOUDS2.JPG. Choose Select➥All and then use the clipboard to copy the image onto a new layer (Layer 1) just above the Clouds layer in the working file. Now choose Layer➥Transform➥Numeric and specify the settings as shown. In the next step, we'll begin to edit these images so that they blend seamlessly with each other as well as the remaining elements of the image.

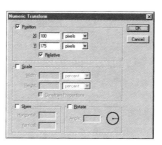

2 Using the Rectangular Marquee tool, define a selection from pixel location (450,100) down to the lower-left extreme (0,1599) of the image window. Hold the (Option)[Alt] key and use the Polygon Lasso tool to subtract from the current selection so that the right border of the resulting selection runs down the center of the god's arm as shown. Now choose Select➡Feather (Radius: 16 pixels). With Layer 1 still active, press the Delete key to help blend the two cloud images. Deselect the selection and then merge down Layer 1 with the Clouds layer. At this point, we'll now move on to correct the top of the clouds image so it naturally blends with the remainder of the image.

3 Choose View➡Zoom Out and then use the Rectangular Marquee tool to define a selection from pixel location (0,0) to (820,1199). Hold the (Option) [Alt] key and then use the Polygon Lasso tool to subtract from the current selection so that the bottom border of the resulting selection follows the contours of the clouds as shown.

4 Now choose View➡Fit on Screen and then save the selection to a new channel (Channel #4). Make Channel #4 active and then make the RGB channel visible so that the image window displays the channel and the image simultaneously. In the next step, we'll edit the channel mask and load it as a selection so that the top edge of the clouds blends with the background.

5 Select the Gradient tool from the toolbox. In the Gradient Tool Options palette, reset the tool and then choose Cancel when prompted. Specify Foreground to Transparent in the Gradient field. Switch to the default colors and then drag out a gradient from pixel location (460,820) to (460,440). Now deselect the selection and then choose Filter➡Blur➡Gaussian Blur (Radius: 12.0 pixels). The channel mask is now complete. In the next step, we'll use it to edit the cloud layer so that it fades more naturally to the background.

6 Load the selection from Channel #4. Now make the RGB channel active and then make Channel #4 invisible. With the Clouds layer still active, press the Delete key twice and then deselect the selection. The cloud layer now fades to the background image and looks very natural.

Finishing Touches

At this point, all of the image elements are in place and the image looks excellent, but there are a few finishing touches that we still need to complete. In the next two steps, we'll add three lens flares before moving on to implement one final step in which we'll soften the appearance of the Roman god. We'll start by adding a lens flare just to the right of the rising arm of the god where the planet drops below the clouds.

1 With the Clouds layer still active, choose Filter➡Render➡Lens Flare (Brightness: 70%, Lens Type: 105 mm Prime) and position the flare as shown. It may take more than one attempt to properly position the flare because you'll have to eyeball the position for the flare within the small preview image of the dialog box. After each attempt, choose Edit➡Undo to remove the flare before implementing additional attempts until you are satisfied with the final appearance.

It's important to note that the position of this flare is more critical than the other flares that will be introduced because we're trying to locate the flare in a region where the opacity of the Clouds layer is diminishing. As a result, the apparent brightness of the flare will vary depending on its exact position. Therefore, you may find it convenient to vary the brightness setting of the flare as well. Now let's move on to add two additional flares to the Background layer.

2 Make the Background layer active and then choose Filter➥Render➥Lens Flare (Brightness: 80%, Lens Type: 35mm Prime) and place the flare as shown. In this case, the placement of the flare is not critical so you most likely won't have to repeat the operation.

Now add the final flare, choose Filter➥Render➥Lens Flare (Brightness: 50%, Lens Type: 105mm Prime) and place the flare as shown.

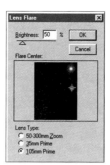

3 Now we'll soften the appearance of the god by blurring its edges. Fantasy images usually have a very soft appearance. Therefore, it's often desirable to blur the edges of prominent objects to produce this effect.

Make the Roman God layer active and then load the layer transparency selection from the layer as well. Choose Select➡ Modify➡Border (16 pixels) and then choose Filter➡Blur➡ Gaussian Blur (Radius: 16 pixels). Now deselect the selection.

At this point the image is complete and looks great. If you wish, choose Layer➡Flatten Image and then save it.

Chapter 10

Changing Day to Night

In Chapter 8, "Using Light to Set the Mood," we used artificial light to create a warm, soft, relaxed appearance in the sample image by reducing the harshness of existing shadows and shifting the color hue towards yellow in the brighter regions. We also used light to emphasize the picture frames as well as the other objects on the glass tabletop by brightening the entire lower portion of the image.

When implementing these modifications, we largely ignored the physical interaction of light with objects in the scene such that the added light did not help to convey any three-dimensional information, such as the relative positions and forms of objects in the scene. Nevertheless, Photoshop can be used to manipulate these qualities to enhance the three-dimensional information that an image conveys and this is exactly what we'll do with the sample image of this technique.

In order to change this lighting condition, we'll actually change the apparent time of day by darkening the image to portray a night scene. In order to complete the effect, we'll have to start by compositing in some light fixtures that will serve as the dominant light sources in the final image. But that's only the beginning. Once the light sources are in place, we'll then move on to create a mask that we'll use to alter the lighting condition of the image. Initially, the mask will be defined such that it respects and enhances the three-dimensional geometry that the image already conveys. We'll then apply the mask using an adjustment layer before we implement an additional modification to demonstrate how light can be used to enhance existing, image detail. More specifically, we'll brighten the plants next to the door in such a way that we actually introduce definition to the individual leaves of the plant.

It's important to note that artificial light is often an ideal form of light with which to enhance the three-dimensional appearance of an image because it exhibits one quality that natural light often does not. More specifically, the brightness of artificial light falls off rapidly with distance from the source, and this characteristic can serve as an additional indicator of the relative position of objects within a scene. In fact, we'll define the mask in such a way that this falloff in brightness is simulated as well.

Altering the Composition

In this case, the quality of the sample image that we'll be working with is already quite good, so there are only a few alterations that need to be completed before we get into the core operations to change the apparent time of day. Most importantly, we'll composite in some lighting fixtures next to the doors. In reality, the entrance that is shown is actually illuminated with flood lights from above the view, but we'll create a more interesting image by introducing lighting fixtures that enhance the image composition. We'll also alter the appearance of the windows in the doors to create a slightly more abstract appearance as well. First, we'll have to skew the image to remove unwanted perspective.

I Open the file named ENTRANCE.TIF.

2 Duplicate the Background layer and then choose View➡Zoom Out. Now choose Layer➡Transform➡Skew and then adjust the lower-left handle downward until the Info palette displays a parallelogram reading of -1.0 degree. Before proceeding, merge down the duplicate layer with the Background layer. In the next step, we'll alter the appearance of the door windows.

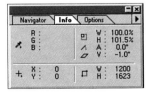

3 Before proceeding, use the Zoom tool to zoom in on the view so that the doors fill the view. Using the Rectangular Marquee tool, define a selection from pixel location (540,347) to (776,655). Now hold the (Option)[Alt] key and then subtract from the current selection by defining a selection from (642,340) to (676,670) and another from (530,515) to (785,546). At this point, all four windows of the door are now selected.

4 With the selection still active, use the clipboard to copy the contents of the selection to a new layer (Layer 1). With Layer 1 now active, turn on the Preserve Transparency option located at the top of the Layers palette. Switch to the default colors and then choose Edit➡Stroke (Width: 8 pixels, Location: Inside, Opacity: 100%). Choose Filter➡Blur➡Gaussian Blur (Radius: 6.0 pixels). Turn off the Preserve Transparency option and then choose Filter➡Blur➡Gaussian Blur (Radius: 1.0 pixels). Now choose Filter➡Noise➡Add Noise (Amount: 6.0, Distribution: Uniform, Monochromatic: Unchecked) and then merge down Layer 1 with the Background layer. In the next step, we'll begin to introduce the lamp into the working image.

5 Open the file named LAMP.PSD. In the Paths palette, make the LAMP PATH active. Choose the Make Selection command from the flyout menu. In the dialog box that now appears, specify a feathering radius 0.5 pixels. Now choose the Turn Off Path command from the flyout menu and then choose Edit➡Copy to copy the contents of the selection to the clipboard. Close the LAMP.TIF file without saving. Now that we're back in the working file, choose View➡Fit on Screen and then choose Edit➡Paste to place the contents of the clipboard onto a new layer (Layer 1). Choose Layer➡Transform➡Numeric and then specify the settings as shown.

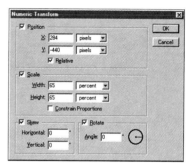

By adjusting the contrast, we were able to draw out the detail of the lamp a bit more, but this also drew out some

6 Choose Image➡Adjust➡Brightness/Contrast (Brightness: 0, Contrast: 30) and then choose Image➡Adjust➡Hue/Saturation (Hue: 20, Saturation: 0, Lightness: 0). Finally, choose Filter➡ Blur➡Gaussian Blur (Radius: 0.3).

continues

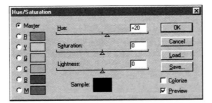

continued

existing red highlights as well as some pixelation. In this case, the highlights were desirable, but the red color and the pixelation were not. By applying the Hue/Saturation adjustments, we were able to alter the color of the highlights to a more suitable color (yellow) and this adjustment improved the appearance of the lamp quite well. The Gaussian Blur filter also helped to soften the appearance of the lamp to eliminate some of the pixelation. Nevertheless, the lamp still has a flat appearance that we'll need to correct, and we'll do this in the next step by adding a layer drop shadow.

7 Make the Background layer active and then create a new layer (Layer 2). With Layer 2 now active, load the layer transparency selection from Layer 1. With the foreground color still set to black, fill the selection with the foreground color and then deselect the selection. Choose Filter➡Blur➡Gaussian Blur (Radius: 6.0 pixels). If the Info palette is not currently visible, choose Window➡Show Info. Now use the Move tool to move the shadow downward and to the right until the Info palette displays a relative pixel position of (3,3). Remember, you may use the Numeric Transform command to complete this task as well. Now we're ready to add in a lamp on the left side of the doorway as well.

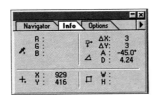

8 Make Layer 1 active and then merge down Layer 1 with Layer 2. Now duplicate Layer 2. With the duplicate layer (Layer 1 copy) now active, choose Layer➡Transform➡Flip Horizontal. Choose View➡Fit on Screen and then use the Move tool to move the duplicate lamp to the left until the Info palette displays a relative pixel position of (-460,0). Once the duplicate lamp is properly placed, merge down the duplicate layer with the Layer 2 and then rename the layer to "Lamps."

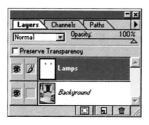

Creating the Mask

At this point, the composition is complete and we're now ready to alter the apparent lighting condition of the image. We'll start by defining a channel mask that we'll then use with an adjustment layer to darken the image in a realistic manner. In other words, we'll define the mask such that the final brightnesses of the individual surfaces are dependent on their apparent orientations with respect to the illuminating sources within the three-dimensional space that the image depicts. More specifically, we'll define the mask such that all surfaces facing away from the light sources (such as the front surfaces of the steps) are darkened more than surfaces that have a direct line of sight to the illuminating lamps. We'll also define the mask to simulate the natural falloff in brightness with distance from the illuminating sources. Once we've altered the brightness of the image, we'll then use the mask to add in some yellow color to create a sense of warmth within the image as well.

I In the Channels palette, create a new channel (Channel #4). Now make the RGB channel visible so that the image window displays the image and the channel simultaneously. Choose the Channel Options command from the flyout menu. In the dialog box that now appears, click the color swatch to change the color to black and then adjust the opacity setting to 80%.

At this point, the image will appear to be darkened. By changing the parameters in the channel options dialog box, the channel mask will now display a more accurate representation of how editing operations will affect the image once the mask is applied with the adjustment layer. In the next several steps, we'll concentrate on the development of the mask. This will require the implementation of several editing operations. Nevertheless, none of the involved operations are difficult to complete, and therefore, we'll proceed with little explanation.

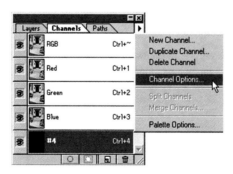

2 If the Info palette isn't currently visible, choose Window➡Show Info and then switch to the default colors. Select the Elliptical Marquee tool from the toolbox and then place the cursor at pixel location (230,160). Now hold the Shift key and then drag out a selection with a pixel width and height of 400 × 400. Press Delete to clear the mask in the selected area.

With the selection still active, place the cursor inside the selection border and then drag the selection to the right until the Info palette displays a relative pixel position of (450,0). Now press Delete once more and then deselect the selection.

3 Using the Rectangular Marquee tool, place the cursor at pixel location (310,210) and drag out a selection to (910,1190). Now hold the Shift key and drag out a selection from (300,500) to (1000,680) and then another from (230,360) to (1078,550).

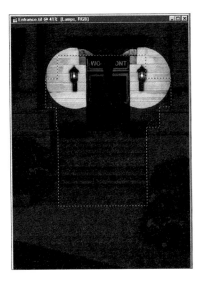

Press Delete and then deselect the selection.

4 Select the Polygon Lasso tool from the toolbox and then define a selection to extend the cleared region so that it follows the contours of the sidewalk on the left. I defined the selection from pixel location (320,870) to (260,1080) to (130,1190) and then to (320,1190) before closing it.

Now that you've defined the selection, press Delete and then deselect the selection. Now we'll edit the right hand side of the mask as well.

5 Using the Polygon Lasso tool, define a selection to edit the mask so that it follows the edge of the flower bed wall on the right. I defined a selection from pixel location (920,980) to (870,1250) and then to (920,1250) before closing it.

At this point, we have a mask that roughly follows the area that we'll want to brighten, but the mask is far from complete. In fact, it must be modified to simulate the natural falloff of brightness with distance from the illuminating sources. In this case, we'll accomplish this in two ways. First, we'll define a gradient across the cleared region so that there is a gradual transition of the cleared region to the masked region in the downward direction. Then we'll blur the mask quite substantially. As you'll soon see, these two operations will make a big difference in the appearance of the mask. However, we'll still need to implement a few editing operations after these modifications are completed before we can apply it with the adjustment layer.

Now switch to the default colors and then fill the selection with the foreground color. Before proceeding, deselect the selection.

6 With channel #4 still active, load the selection from the channel as well. Now select the Gradient tool from the toolbox. In the Gradient Tool Options palette, reset the tool. Switch to the default colors and then switch the foreground and background colors. Now set the foreground color to gray (R: 120 G: 120 B: 120). Place the cursor along the edge between the top step and the surface of the porch and then drag out a gradient to the bottom edge of the selection. I defined the gradient from pixel location (650,770) to (650,1180).

Now deselect the selection and then choose
Filter➡Blur➡Gaussian Blur (Radius: 40 pixels).

At this point, the mask is starting to look excellent. The operations of this step, however,
extended the cleared region
into areas where it should not
exist. Most notably, some of the
wall surfaces that are facing
completely away from the light
sources have been brightened a
bit, and so we'll have to implement a few corrections to dark-
en these regions before we can
use the mask. The front surfaces of the steps also need to
be darkened, which we'll do as
well.

7 Using the Rectangular Marquee tool, place the cursor at pixel
location (925,706) and then drag out a selection to the bottom
right corner of the image at (1199,1599). Now hold the Shift key
and define a selection from (1009,565) to (1199,690), another
from (1010,565) to (1199,582), and another from (1091,570) to
the extreme, upper right corner of the image at (1199,0).

Choose Select➥Feather (Radius: 2.0 pixels). With the background color still set to black, press Delete and then deselect the selection. Now we'll move on to complete the walls on the left hand side of the image as well.

8 Using the Rectangular Marquee tool, place the cursor at pixel location (260,704) and then drag out a selection to (0,1000). Now hold the Shift key and define a selection from (253,565) to (0,683), and another from (173,570) to (0,0).

Choose Select➡Feather (Radius: 2.0 pixels). With the background color still set to black, press Delete and then deselect the selection. Now we'll move on to complete the steps in front of the doorway.

9 Using the Polygon Lasso tool, define a selection that isolates the front surfaces of the top step. Now hold the Shift key and define additional selections to create a composite selection that isolates all of the steps.

Before proceeding, choose View➡Fit On Screen. Now choose Select➡Feather (Radius: 3.0 pixels) and then set the foreground color to dark gray (R: 40 G: 40 B: 40). Fill the selection with the foreground color and then deselect the selection.

Adjusting the Lighting

At this point, the mask is complete and we can now use it to create an adjustment layer that selectively darkens the pixels of the image. As already mentioned, we'll also use the mask to add in some yellow color to the brightened areas to create a sense of warmth as well. Once we've completed these changes, we'll then have no further need to use the mask, but we will move on to implement additional changes. Most notably, we'll add in some color to make the lamps appear to shine more brightly.

1 Make the RGB channel active and then make channel #4 invisible. Now load the selection from Channel #4 and choose OK when prompted. Invert the selection. In the Layers palette, choose the New Adjustment Layer command from the flyout menu. In the dialog box that appears, name the new layer Adjustment and then specify Hue/Saturation as the type. In the next dialog box that appears, adjust the settings to (Hue: 0, Saturation: 0, Lightness: -80). As you can see, the adjustment looks just like the mask. The image, however, has a cold appearance so we'll add in some yellow to the brightened regions to warm things up a bit.

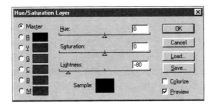

Because none of the pixels are more than 50% selected, it is important that you not forget to deselect the selection that is active.

2 In the Channels palette, load the selection from channel #4 once again and choose OK when prompted. In the Layers palette, create a new layer and name it Warmth. Set the foreground color to pale yellow (R: 255 G: 215 B: 130) and then fill the selection with the foreground color. Deselect the selection. Now change the layer apply mode to Overlay and then adjust the layer opacity to 70%. Now we'll adjust the apparent brightness of the light sources by adding some additional color over the glass panes of the light fixtures.

3 Before proceeding, select the Zoom tool from the toolbox and then zoom in on the view so that the right lamp dominates the view. Create a new layer named Lamp Light. Using the Polygon Lasso tool, define a selection that isolates the front glass pane of the lamp. Now hold the Shift key and define additional selections to create a composite selection that isolates the two side panes as well. With the foreground color still set to pale yellow, fill the selection with the foreground color and then deselect the selection. In the next step, we'll modify the newly added color to create a glowing appearance.

4 Choose Filter➡Blur➡Gaussian Blur (Radius: 4.0 pixels) and then choose Image➡Adjust➡Hue/Saturation. In the dialog box that appears, turn on the Colorize option and then adjust the settings to (Hue: +55, Saturation: 100, Lightness: +10). Now duplicate the layer. With the duplicate (Lamp Light copy) active, change the layer apply mode to Overlay and then adjust the layer opacity to 70%. Now merge down the duplicate layer with the Lamp Light layer. In the next step, we'll complete the left lamp as well.

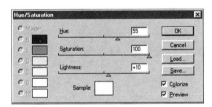

As you can see, this enhances the appearance of the image, but one more modification still needs to be completed. We'll add a halo of light around the lamp where the back wall would reflect its light because of the wall's proximity to the lamp.

5 Before proceeding, choose View➡Fit On screen. Duplicate the Lamp Light layer and then use the Move tool to move the duplicate image so that it is centered over the left lamp. I moved the duplicate until the Info palette displayed a relative position of (-460,0). Now merge down the duplicate layer (Lamp Light copy) with the Lamp Light layer.

6 Create a new layer and name it Light Halo. Using the Elliptical Marquee tool, place the cursor at pixel location (800,250) and then drag out a selection to (960,480).

With the foreground color still set to yellow, fill the selection with the foreground color and then deselect the selection. Now choose Filter➡Blur➡Gaussian Blur (Radius: 30 pixels). Change the layer apply mode to Overlay and then adjust the layer opacity to 50%.

At this point, the local region around the lamp looks natural and the halo enhances the appearance quite nicely. In the next step, we'll duplicate the halo to complete the left lamp as well.

Now we need to brighten the plants next to the door. In fact, we'll do this by enhancing the apparent detail of the plants by brightening the leaves of the plant individually.

7 Now duplicate the Light Halo layer and then use the Move tool to move the duplicate image to the left so that it is centered over the left lamp. I moved the duplicate until the Info palette displayed a relative position of (-460,0). Now merge down the duplicate layer (Light Halo copy) with the Light Halo layer.

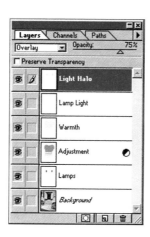

8 Select the Paintbrush tool from the toolbox. In the Brushes palette, select the New Brush command from the flyout menu. In the dialog box that now appears, adjust the settings to (Diameter: 7 pixels, Hardness: 100%, Spacing: 110%). The purpose of these settings will be explained in the next step.

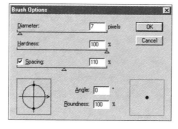

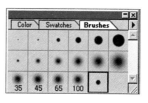

9 In the Layers palette, make the Adjustment layer active. Switch to the default colors and then switch the foreground and background colors. Now use the Paintbrush tool to stroke over the plants next to the doorway. As you proceed, make sure to follow the contours of the plants as closely as possible.

Once you have complete both plants, choose Filter➥Blur➥ Gaussian Blur (Radius: 1.0 pixels). At this point, the image is complete. If you wish, flatten the image before saving it. It is also recommended that you apply the Water Color filter to add a more artistic style to the image.

As you can see, this creates a very natural appearance that enhances the detail of the plant quite nicely. The diameter of the brush is chosen to match the approximate size of each individual leaf and the spacing is chosen to produce distinct dots to simulate a more natural texture. The hardness of the brush is also chosen to provide the greatest amount of flexibility to complete the effect. In other words, the hard brush produces more detail than what would have been achieved with a soft brush. As you can see, the amount of apparent detail can also easily be lowered afterwards by applying the Gaussian Blur filter. In this case, notice that we applied the blur filter to the entire image, which is completely acceptable, because the mask had previously been blurred with a much higher setting.

Introducing an Artistic Style

At this point, the image is complete and looks excellent, but I'd like to take the opportunity to demonstrate how you can introduce an artistic style to many of the final images that you produce in Photoshop. In this case, we'll be introducing a watercolor effect. As you may already know, Photoshop provides an artistic filter called the Watercolor filter, but I rarely apply the artistic filters without implementing some supplemental operations that provide more control over the amount of image detail that is retained in the final image, which is what we'll do here.

Before proceeding, save the existing image, if you wish, and then choose Image➡Duplicate. In the dialog box that appears, turn on the Merged Layers Only option. With the duplicate image now active, duplicate the Background layer. With the duplicate layer (Background copy) now active, choose Filter➡Artistic➡ Watercolor (Brush Detail: 8, Shadow Intensity: 1, Texture: 1) and then choose Filter➡Blur➡Gaussian Blur (Radius: 0.5 pixels). Now choose Filter➡Stylize➡Diffuse (Mode: Normal). Adjust the layer opacity to 70% and then choose Layer➡Flatten Image. In this case, we used the Gaussian Blur filter to soften the effect that the Watercolor filter produces and then we reduced the layer opacity to re-introduce some of the original image detail to produce the final appearance.

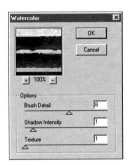

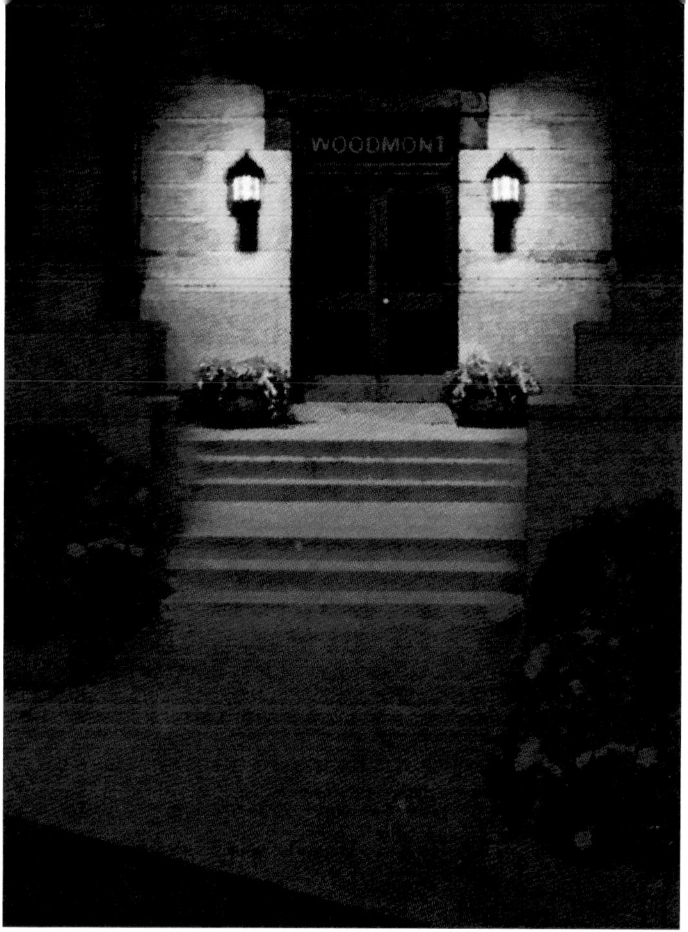
WOODMONT

Chapter 11

Working with a Central Theme

One of the great things about Photoshop is that you can use it to combine image elements in such a way that the composite image defies reality. In fact, that's exactly what we'll accomplish in this technique, and we'll do it by creating an image that displays a waterfall pouring from the screen of a high definition television set. But the great thing about this image isn't so much that it defies reality; it's that the image presents a central theme which the viewer can easily identify. By identifying the central theme, the viewer is presented with a message. In fact, the sample image of this technique would make a great advertisement for high definition television, because it conveys the idea that the television picture is so clear that the image appears to be real and, in this case, results in the flow of water out of the screen.

Preparing the Television Set

In the final image that we seek, the television set plays a central role. Therefore, it should come as no surprise that we'll begin by preparing the image of the television set, which we'll then begin to integrate with the waterfall image in the next section. In this case, our goal is to produce a very clean-looking, high definition television set, and we'll actually use Photoshop as a painting program to produce the image from an ordinary photograph of a standard television set.

1 Open the file named TV.PSD. If the guides are not displayed, choose View➡Show Guides. I've placed several guides to help speed up the development of the television image. It's important to note that the positions of all the guides are placed to mark the significant points of the television image and to be completely symmetric about the vertical centerline that I've marked with a guide as well. As a result, the critical points that the guides are used to mark may not line up exactly with the source image on the Background layer, which exhibits some optical distortions.

In the Layers palette, you'll notice that I've also provided the final image on the HDTV layer that I produced by following the steps of this section. If you wish to skip this section, feel free to use this image by simply renaming the Final Image layer to HDTV and then moving on to the next section, "Introducing the Television Picture." In the Paths palette, you'll notice that I've also provided you with three predefined paths, and we'll start with the development of the television image with the Screen path in the next step.

As with all of the other image elements that we're about to introduce, it's important to note that I used guides to accurately place the defining points of the Screen path to ensure that the final result was accurate and symmetrical about the vertical centerline. Once the defining points were all in place, I then edited the top- and bottom-center points of the path by dragging out the tensions of those points along the horizontal guides that were used to mark their locations. These guides have since been removed to prevent the image from appearing overly cluttered.

2 Create a new layer named Screen. In the Paths palette, make the SCREEN PATH active and then choose the Make Selection command from the flyout menu. In the dialog box that now appears, specify a feathering radius of 0.5 pixels. Now choose the Turn Off Path command from the flyout menu as well. Switch to the default colors and then fill the selection with the foreground color. Deselect the selection.

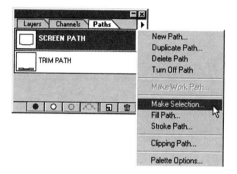

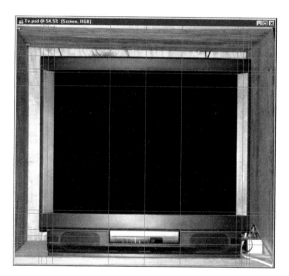

3 Make the Background layer active and then create a new layer named Frame. Using the Rectangular Marquee tool, define a selection from pixel location (135,215) to (1165,920) and then choose Select→Feather (Radius: 0.5 pixel). Now set the foreground color to dark gray (R: 20 G: 20 B: 20) and then fill the selection with the foreground color. Deselect the selection.

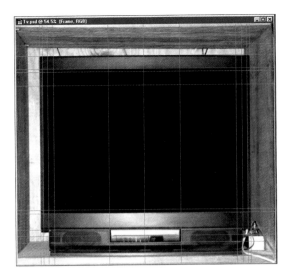

Using the Polygon Lasso tool, define a selection from pixel location (135,215) to (190,230) to (190,905) to (135,920) and then close the selection. Now hold the Shift key and add to the selection by defining another selection from pixel location (1110,230) to (1165,215) to (1165,920) to (1110,905) and then close the selection. Now choose Select➡Feather (Radius: 0.5 pixels). Set the foreground color to gray (R: 60 G: 70 B: 70) and then fill the selection with the foreground color. Deselect the selection.

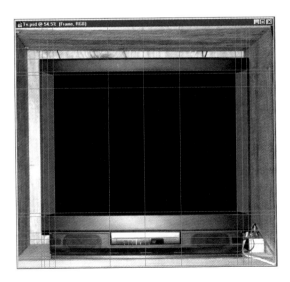

4 Make the Background layer active and then create a new layer named TV Case. Using the Rectangular Marquee tool, define a selection from pixel location (120,150) to (1180,1000). Now choose Select➥Modify➥Smooth (8 pixels) and then choose Select➥Feather (Radius: 0.5 pixels). Now set the foreground color to dark gray (R: 30 G: 30 B: 30) and then fill the selection with the foreground color. We'll continue to use the selection in the next step.

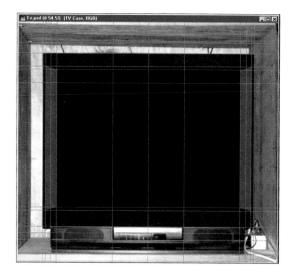

5 With the selection still active, create a new layer (Layer 1). Using the Rectangular Marquee tool, place the cursor at pixel location (650,100). Now hold the (Option)[Alt] key and drag out a selection to the lower right corner of the image at pixel location (1299,1169) to eliminate the right hand side of the existing selection.

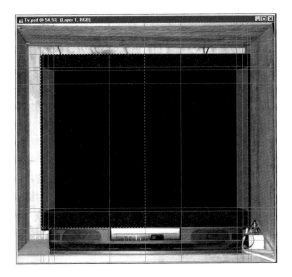

Now select the Gradient tool from the toolbox. In the Gradient Tool Options palette, reset the tool and then choose Cancel when prompted. Specify Transparent to Foreground in the Gradient field. Now switch the foreground and background colors and then drag out a gradient from pixel location (190,215) to (650,215). Deselect the selection.

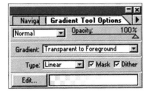

In the next step we'll reflect a duplicate of this gradient to complete the right hand side of the television. We'll then make an opacity adjustment to provide a subtle highlight across the case of the television to simulate a more contoured surface that is slightly bowed along its center. Real television sets usually exhibit smooth contours and gradual variations in much the same way, and the addition of this surface gradient will help to enhance the three-dimensional appearance of the appliance.

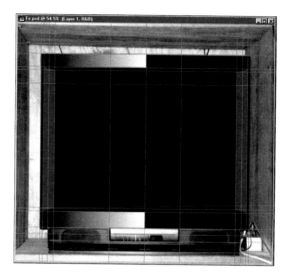

6 Duplicate Layer 1. With the duplicate layer (Layer 1 copy) now active, choose Layer➥Transform➥Flip Horizontal and then choose Layer➥Transform➥Numeric. In the dialog box that now appears, specify a relative position of (229,0) and disable all other input fields before applying. Merge down the duplicate layer with Layer 1 and then adjust the layer opacity to 30%. Now merge down Layer 1 with the TV Case layer. With the TV Case layer now active, link the Frame and Screen layers to the TV Body Layer and then merge the linked layers.

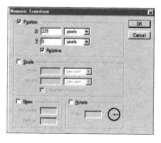

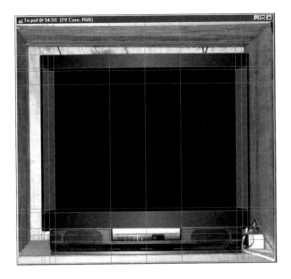

7 Make the Background layer active. Using the Rectangular Marquee tool, define a selection from pixel location (470,1000) to (830,1065). Choose Select➡Modify➡Smooth (4 pixels) and then choose Select➡Feather (Radius: 0.5 pixels). Now use the clipboard to copy the contents of the selection to a new layer and rename it to Control Panel. Choose Image➡Adjust➡ Hue/Saturation. In the dialog box that now appears, turn on the Colorize option and then adjust the settings to (Hue: 180, Saturation: 10, Lightness: -55). Now choose Image➡Adjust➡ Brightness/Contrast (Brightness: 0, Contrast: -25).

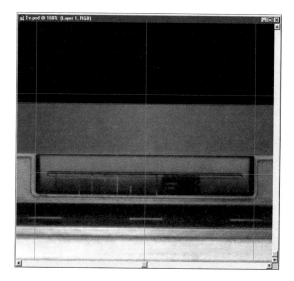

8 Create a new layer (Layer 1). Select the Line tool from the toolbox. In the Line Tool Options palette, specify a width of 4 pixels. Now set the foreground color to dark gray (R: 35 G: 40 B: 40) and then draw lines over the individual grooves that define the buttons of the control panel. If necessary, use the Undo command and/or the Eraser tool to eliminate mistakes. Once you're done and satisfied with the result, choose Filter➡Blur➡Gaussian Blur (Radius: 0.3 pixels) and then merge down Layer 1 with the Control Panel layer.

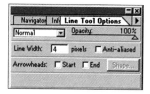

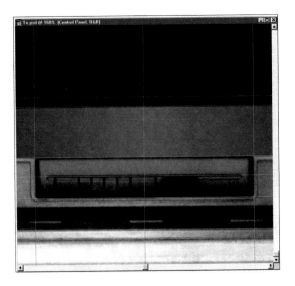

9 Make the Background layer active and then create a new layer named TV Stand. Using the Rectangular Marquee tool, define a selection from pixel location (160,1000) to (1140,1115). Now choose Select➡Modify➡Smooth (8 pixels) and then choose Select➡Feather (Radius: 0.5 pixels). With the foreground color still set to gray (R: 35 G: 40 B: 40), fill the selection with the foreground color and then deselect the selection.

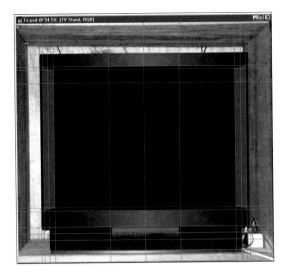

Using the Rectangular Marquee tool, define a new selection from pixel location (160,1115) to (1140,1130). Choose

At this point, the stand has a very flat and uninteresting appearance. In the next several steps, we'll add some shadows and highlights to add visual interest and create a more three-dimensional appearance for the stand.

Select➡Modify➡Smooth (8 pixels) and then choose Select➡ Feather (Radius: 0.5 pixels). Now fill the selection with the foreground color and then deselect the selection. Before proceeding, choose View➡Hide Guides. They are no longer needed.

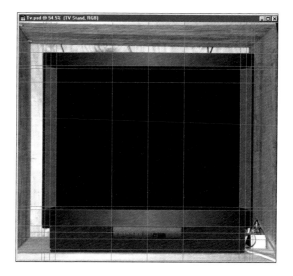

10 Select the Paintbrush tool from the toolbox. In the Brushes palette, select the New Brush command from the flyout menu. In the dialog box that now appears, adjust the settings to (Diameter: 5 pixels, Hardness: 0%, Spacing: 25%).

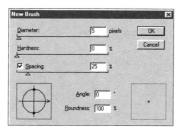 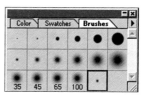

11 In the Layers palette, make the Control Panel layer active and then create a new layer (Layer 1). Now switch to the default colors. In the Paths palette, make the TRIM PATH active and then choose the Stroke Path command from the flyout menu. In the dialog box that now appears, specify the Paintbrush as the tool. Now choose the Turn Off Path command from the flyout menu as well.

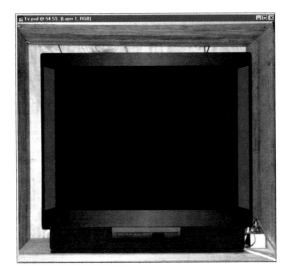

Select the Line tool from the toolbox. In the Line Tool Options palette, reset the tool and then specify a width of 8 pixels. Now draw a line from pixel location (168,1000) to (1132,1000). Choose Filter➥Blur➥Gaussian Blur (Radius: 2.5 pixels). Before proceeding, choose View➥Hide Guides. At this point, the guides are no longer required.

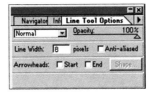

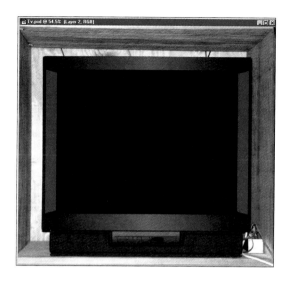

12 Create a new layer (Layer 2) and then select the Line tool from the toolbox. Switch the foreground and background colors. In the Line Tool Options palette, set the line width to 4 pixels, draw a line from pixel location (168,1115) to (1132,1115), and then choose Filter➡Blur➡Gaussian Blur (Radius: 2.5 pixels). Now adjust the layer opacity to 30%.

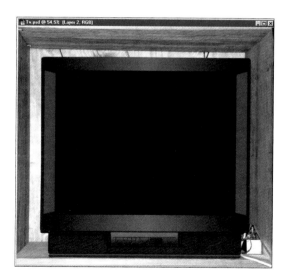

13 Make the TV Stand layer active and then link all of the other layers except the Background layer and the Final Image layers. Now merge the linked layers. Rename the resulting layer to TV SET. Now duplicate the TV SET layer and rename the duplicate layer to HDTV. Choose Layer➡Transform➡Scale and then move the top-center handle of the Transformation tool downward until the Info palette displays a scale factor of 80% for the height.

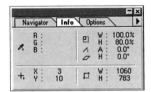

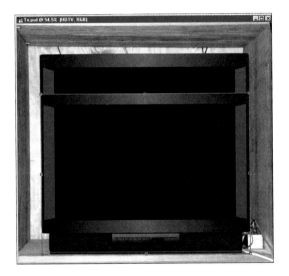

Introducing the Television Picture

At this point, the TV set looks great, but we still need to introduce an appropriate image to the screen of the TV, and we'll do this before we copy the TV set to the waterfall image. In this case, we'll introduce the image to the screen of the HDTV with the help of a layer mask to properly limit the display of the image. But first, there are a few operations that we need to implement to edit the image.

We'll be using an image taken in the Azore Islands of Portugal, which is chosen because of the large body of water that is depicted in the foreground. In fact, we could have used almost any image with this feature.

I Open the file named TV_IMAGE.PSD. Using the Rectangular Marquee tool, place the cursor at pixel location (0,360) and drag out a selection to the lower-right hand corner at (1023,767). In the Paths palette, make the BOAT PATH active and then choose the Make Selection command from the flyout menu. In the dialog box that now appears, specify a feathering radius of 4 pixels and then turn on the Subtract from Selection option. Now choose the Turn Off Path command from the flyout menu as well.

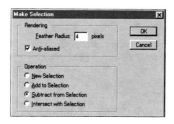

I used the Motion Blur filter to slightly smooth the appearance of the water. This will help to ensure that the image will blend more naturally when it is eventually integrated with the waterfall in a later step.

2 Choose Filter➡Blur➡Motion Blur (Angle: 0 degrees, Distance: 10 pixels) and then deselect the selection. Now choose Select➡All and then choose Edit➡Copy to place the contents of the selection to the clipboard. If you wish, save the changes to the file and then close the file as well.

3 Now that we're back in the TV.PSD image, make the HDTV SCREEN PATH active. Now choose the Make Selection command from the Paths palette flyout menu. In the dialog box that now appears, specify a feathering radius of 0.5 pixels. With the image from the TV_IMAGE.PSD file still in the clipboard, press (Command+Shift+V)[Control+Shift+V] to place the contents of the clipboard onto a new layer (Layer 1) with a layer mask created from the active selection. Merge down Layer 1 with the HDTV layer and save the file. Before proceeding, choose Select➡All and then choose Edit➡Copy to place the contents of the selection in the clipboard. Now close the file without saving.

Integrating the Television with the Waterfall Image

Now that we've integrated the landscape image with the TV image, we can now move along to integrate the television with the waterfall image to produce the final, composite image. This will require some major changes to the composition of the waterfall image that we'll implement after we paste the TV into the image. First, we need to place a few guides that will help us to integrate the television image more easily.

1 Open the file named WATER.TIF. Choose View➡Show Rulers and then place a vertical guide at pixel location 357 and another at 933. Now place a horizontal guide at 435. These guides frame the outline of the waterfall and we'll rely on them quite heavily as we proceed.

2 With the television image still in the clipboard, choose Edit➡Paste to place the image onto a new layer and then rename the layer to Television. Choose Layer➡Transform➡Numeric and specify the settings as shown. Now place a horizontal guide along the bottom edge of the television at pixel location 804. This guide should snap right into place.

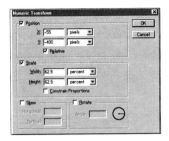

3 Make the Background layer active. Using the Rectangular Marquee tool, define a selection from pixel location (0,435) to (1399,1275). Now use the clipboard to copy the contents of the selection to a new layer (Layer 1) and then rename the layer to Concrete Ledge. Choose Layer➡Transform➡Scale and then move the top-center handle of the transformation tool downward until the Info palette displays a scale factor of 56.0% for the height. In the Layers palette, now move the Concrete Ledge layer above the Television layer.

In this case, you'll notice that there is a brown water stain that tapers inward towards the top of the waterfall on both sides. In fact, the image on the current layer was scaled down so that the water stain appears to taper inward before reaching the ledge upon which the television will appear to sit in the final image. By scaling the image, we actually prevent the stain from being cut off abruptly at the ledge, but we've also altered the falling water which now appears to be flowing from the base of the television

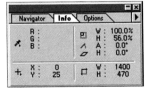

continues

continued

*instead of the television screen.
Therefore, we'll have to correct
this circumstance which we'll
do in Step 5, but first we'll
implement a few operations to
create a more prominent
appearance for the ledge. More
specifically, we'll duplicate the
top edge of the wall on the
right to provide a more natural
looking edge for the ledge as
well.*

4 Make the Background layer active. With the Rectangular
Marquee tool still selected, define a selection from pixel location
(933,170) to (1399,250) and then choose Select➡Feather
(Radius: 1.0 pixels). Use the clipboard to copy the contents of the
selection to a new layer (Layer 1). In the Layers palette, move
Layer 1 above the Concrete Ledge layer and then use the Move
tool to move the image on Layer 1 downward until the Info
palette displays a relative pixel position of (-1,639).

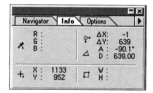

5 The duplicate image should snap right into place along both the horizontal and vertical guides. Now use the Rectangular Marquee tool to define another selection from pixel location (900,840) to (1399,1000). Choose Select➡Feather (Radius: 16 pixels) and then press Delete twice to create a more gradual transition along the bottom edge of the duplicate ledge to the underlying image. Deselect the selection.

6 Duplicate Layer 1. With the duplicate layer (Layer 1 copy) now active, choose Layer➡Transform➡Flip Horizontal and then use the Move tool to move the duplicate image of the ledge to the left until the Info palette displays a relative pixel position of (-1042,0). Now merge down Layer 1 copy with Layer 1 and then merge down Layer 1 with the Concrete Ledge layer.

The ledge is now complete. In the next step, we'll begin to make the necessary corrections to make the water appear to be flowing out from the image displayed on the television screen. Before proceeding, choose View➡Hide Guides. They are no longer needed to complete the remaining operations of this technique.

7 Using the Rectangular Marquee tool, define a selection from pixel location (357,804) to (933,1280). Now use the clipboard to copy the contents of the selection to a new layer (Layer 1) and then rename the new layer to Waterfall. If the image on the Waterfall layer is offset, use the Move tool to realign it with the underlying image. In this case, the existing guides should cause the image to snap back to its proper position. Now choose Layer➡Transform➡Scale and move the top-center handle of the transformation tool upward until the Info palette displays a scale factor of 130.0% for the height.

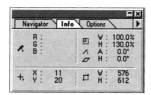

8 Duplicate the Waterfall layer. With the duplicate layer (Waterfall copy) now active, make the Waterfall layer invisible. Now use the Rectangular Marquee tool to define a selection from pixel location (300,435) to (1000,804) and then press Delete to remove the very top of the waterfall image on the duplicate layer. In the Layers palette, move the duplicate layer below the Waterfall layer and then merge down the duplicate layer with the Concrete Ledge layer. Before proceeding, choose View➡Hide Rulers and then choose View➡Hide Guides. Neither of these features are needed as we proceed.

9 Now make the Waterfall layer active. Choose Image➡Adjust➡Desaturate and then adjust the layer opacity to 50%. Now choose Image➡Adjust➡Hue/Saturation. In the dialog box that appears, turn on the Colorize option and then adjust the settings to (Hue: 180, Saturation: 20, Lightness: 0). Now choose Image➡Adjust➡Brightness/Contrast (Brightness: 30, Contrast: 15). Using the Rectangular Marquee tool, define a selection from pixel location (300,550) to (1000,672) and then choose Select➡Feather (Radius: 8 pixels). Now press Delete to create a more natural transition of the waterfall to the television screen image.

The waterfall and the concrete ledge both look great, and they are complete. However, we still need to clean up the image on the background layer to remove the original waterfall as well as the water stains that appear above the ledge in the image. We'll also change the composition so that the image displays a solid wall behind the television set. In fact, we'll accomplish all of these goals by simply making multiple copies of the right wall and then moving the copies to cover the unwanted elements in the background.

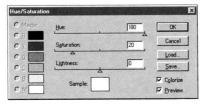

10 Make the Background layer active. Using the Rectangular Marquee tool, define a selection from pixel location (1100,190) to (1370,790) and then choose Select➡Feather (Radius: 16 pixels). Use the clipboard to copy the contents of the selection to a new layer (Layer 1). Now use the Move tool to move the image on Layer 1 until the Info palette displays a relative pixel location of (-300,30).

Now duplicate Layer 1 and move the duplicate to another location that needs covering. Continue to make duplicates of Layer 1 until you have produced a single, solid wall behind the television set. Once you're done, merge down Layer 1 as well as all the other duplicate layers to the Background layer.

Although the image is coming together quite nicely, it looks a bit flat. We can enhance the three-dimensional appearance of the image by creating a shadow behind the television set, and we'll do this in the next step.

11 With the Background layer still active, create a new layer named TV Shadow. Load the layer transparency selection from the Television layer and then choose Select➡Modify➡Expand (4 pixels). Switch to the default colors and then fill the selection with the foreground color. Deselect the selection. Now choose Filter➡Blur➡Gaussian Blur (Radius: 20 pixels) and then adjust the layer opacity to 80%.

Adding the Flowers

At this point, the image is almost complete. In fact, we only have one more element that needs to be introduced to complete the image. In this case, the additional element is a bed of flowers which will help to add some color into the image.

1 Open the file named FLOWERS.PSD. In the Paths palette, make PATH 1 active and then choose the Make Selection command from the flyout menu. In the dialog box that now appears, specify a feathering radius of 0.5 pixels. Now choose the Turn Off Path command from the flyout menu and then choose Edit➡Copy to place the contents of the selection in the clipboard. Close the FLOWERS.PSD file without saving.

2 Now that you are back in the working image, make the Background layer active and then choose Edit➡Paste to place the contents of the clipboard onto a new layer (Layer 1). Rename Layer 1 to Flowers. Now choose Layer➡Transform➡Numeric and specify the settings as shown. In the Layers palette, duplicate the Flowers layer and then move the duplicate layer (Flowers copy) to the right until the Info palette displays a relative pixel position of (1250,0). Now merge down the duplicate layer with the Flowers layer.

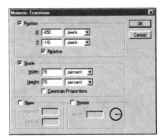

3 Duplicate the Flowers layer. In the Layers palette, move the duplicate layer (Flowers copy) to the top of the stack. Now use the Move tool to move the image on the duplicate layer upward and to the left until the Info palette displays a relative pixel position of (-20,-140). In the next step we'll add a shadow behind the flowers in the same way that we added a shadow behind the television. Then we'll complete the image by cropping it to its final size.

4 Create a new layer named Flowers Shadow. In the Layers palette, move the new layer below the Flowers Copy layer. Now load the layer transparency selection from the Flowers copy layer and then choose Select➡Modify➡Expand (4 pixels). With the foreground color still set to black, fill the selection with the foreground color. Deselect the selection. Now choose Filter➡Blur➡Gaussian Blur (Radius: 20 pixels) and then adjust the layer opacity to 50%. Now choose Layer➡Flatten Image and then select the crop tool from the toolbox. Place the cursor at pixel location (50,150) and drag out the cropping border to a width and height of 1200 × 1600 pixels before applying.

Chapter 12

Web Graphics: Creating an Animated Gear System

Cowritten with Sebastien Lienard

There's no question that Photoshop has made enormous contributions to the visual content that makes the web a more interesting place to visit. These days people expect to see high-quality graphics that enhance the basic information most web pages are designed to present. The fact of the matter is that we're all used to the slick marketing that permeates almost every medium including television, magazines, and yes, even the web. However, the web imposes severe limitations on how graphics can be displayed. Therefore it's no surprise that many web designers turn to powerful applications like Photoshop to work more effectively within the web's limitations.

In fact, Photoshop is becoming more web friendly with each new release. With the introduction of version 3.0, Adobe introduced support for the transparent, interlaced GIF format, which is now one of the most popular formats for graphics on the web. In the latest release, Photoshop now supports several more web-related formats and includes a new feature called Actions. While the Actions feature isn't explicitly a web-related capability, it is a convenient tool that web page designers can use to leverage the capabilities of the application to ultimately increase their productivity. In fact, this new feature makes it possible to produce graphics that were previously too complicated to reasonably complete with Photoshop, and the sample animation of this chapter is no exception.

In this chapter, we'll produce a GIF animation that consists of three rotating gears. In order to complete the animation, each gear must be recreated from several basic components for each of the 60 frames that we'll produce to complete the animation. As you'll soon see, this is no small feat. In fact, no less than eight layers and seven channels will have to be rotated between each frame. In order to create the final, 3-D appearance of the gears, we'll also have to create layer drop shadows and apply the Lighting Effects filter seven times for each frame. All of this is complicated even further by the fact that each gear has a different rate of rotation. Can you imagine having to keep track of all these items over 60 frames? If it weren't for the Actions capability, I don't know of too many people who would be crazy enough to attempt such a complicated project.

Importing the Gear Outlines

In this technique, our starting point is provided by a gear system that was designed in AutoCAD using the Advanced Modeling Extension of Release 12. After the gear system was designed, each gear was then exported to its own EPS-formatted file so that the individual gears could be imported into Photoshop to provide us with their basic outlines. We'll then add textures to these outlines before performing the remaining steps to animate the entire system. In the steps of this section, not only will we import the individual gears, but we'll also implement a few editing operations to make them easier to work with before proceeding to other tasks.

1 Create a new file with pixel dimensions of 2000 x 2000 at 72 dpi in the Grayscale mode and name it GEARS.PSD. This is the file in which we'll be constructing the animation. In fact, we'll start by loading the EPS-formatted files that define the outlines of the individual gears in the system. Once these outlines are in place and edited, we'll then resample the image to 1000 × 1000 at 72 dpi before introducing the background, the gear textures, and some global lighting parameters.

The final animation will then be constructed from this file to produce individual frames with a final frame sizes of 300 × 300 at 72 dpi. By using these larger images up front, we are able to produce a higher quality animation.

Before we begin, it's important to note that the CD-ROM provides all the working files that I used to create the final animation. Among these files is the SYSTEM.PSD file, which contains the basic components of the gear system. The CD-ROM also contains the SYSTEM.ATN file, which was written specifically to be used with the SYSTEM.PSD file. These are essentially the same files (with some minor variations for the sake of performance instead of clarity) that the first three sections of this technique will tell you how to construct. Therefore, it's not necessary that you construct these files to produce the final animation, but you should follow through the individual steps of these sections to gain an understanding of how everything is done.

Once you've completed these sections, you'll have all the knowledge you need to easily understand the setup of the working file that I used to complete the final animation (even with the minor variations that exist). Refer to the section titled "Playing the Action and Generating the Frames" for explicit information on how to use the two files.

2 Before you place the first gear, choose View➡Fit on Screen to maximize the image window. Also, choose File➡Preferences➡ General and then make sure that the Anti-alias Postscript option is turned on. At this point, it's important that you not resize the image window or alter the view in any way until all of the gears have been placed into the file.

Now choose File➡Place and then select the file named GEAR1A.EPS. When the gear image appears in the image window, press Enter to accept the default size and placement so that the image is placed on a new layer named Gear1a.eps.

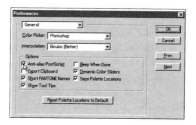

At this point, the gear outline that is displayed will most likely have a very faded appearance and its borders may not appear to be solid. In the next step, we'll stroke the outlines of the gears to make them more visible, but we first need to place the remaining gears of the system. Repeat the File➡Place command to introduce the remaining gears from the files named GEAR1B.EPS, GEAR2.EPS, and GEAR3.EPS. As you proceed, make sure to accept the default sizes and positions for each of the gears to create three new layers named Gear1b.eps, Gear2.eps, Gear3.eps.

Now that the outlines are all in place, feel free to change the view using the Zoom tool to inspect the outlines more closely. Upon doing so, you'll notice that all of the outlines are actually solid lines. As we move along through the steps of this technique, we'll make extensive use of these outlines to select the individual regions of the gears. These outlines will also appear in the final animation to help define the geometry of the gears more clearly. At this point, the outlines are too faint to be used practically for either of these two purposes. Therefore, we'll implement operations in the next two steps to make them more visible before proceeding on to other tasks.

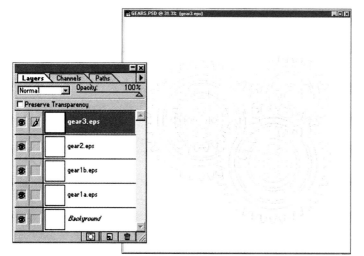

3 Select the Magic Wand tool from the toolbox. In the Magic Wand Options palette, reset the tool and then specify a tolerance of 4 pixels. Before proceeding, make the Gear1a layer active and then make the other gear layers invisible. In the next step, we'll use the Magic Wand tool to define selections that we'll then stoke to darken the outlines that already exist.

In the accompanying image, the resulting selection is displayed as a mask so that you can more readily see which areas of the gear should now be selected. Keep in mind that the masked (red) areas are the regions that are not selected. As we proceed with this technique, selections will often be displayed as masks because many of the selections that we'll be defining are not discernible when displayed as selections. If you want, you can temporarily enter Quick Mask mode each time you define a selection to compare your selection more directly with the masks that are displayed in the accompanying images. Refer to the basic operations chapter for more information on how to enter Quick Mask mode.

4 Using the Magic Wand tool, select the outermost region of the gear and then work towards the center by selecting every second, concentric region as indicated in the accompanying image.

5 Switch to the default colors. Now choose Edit➡Stroke (Width: 4 pixels, Location: Inside, Opacity: 100%) and then deselect the selection.

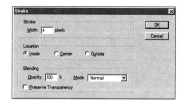

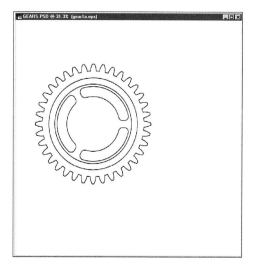

6 Now repeat the operations of the previous step to stroke the outlines on each successive layer until you complete all of the gears in the system. As you proceed to each new layer, make the new layer active and then make all the other Gear*.eps layers invisible.

When using the Magic Wand tool to select the regions of each gear, you should always proceed in the same fashion, starting with the outermost region of the gear and then working towards the center by selecting every second, concentric region. It's important to make the selections in this manner to prevent borders from being double-stroked. To avoid confusion, refer to the corresponding images that display the correct selections as masks for each of the remaining gears.

Up until now, it was acceptable to work in the Grayscale mode because the outlines do not exhibit any color, but we'll now begin to introduce a colored texture for the background. We'll also be introducing and maintaining several new layers for each gear in the system. Therefore, the size of the file

continues

7 Once you complete all the gears, make the Background layer active and then make all the gear#.eps layers visible. Choose Image➡Image Size and then specify new pixel dimensions of 1000 × 1000 to reduce the image to half its current size. Now choose Image➡Mode➡RGB mode and then choose Don't Flatten when prompted.

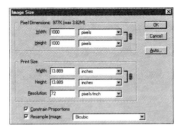

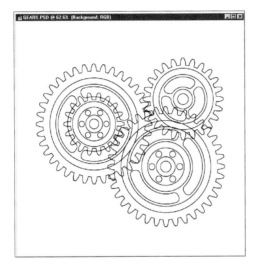

continued

has been reduced to make the task more manageable. Nevertheless, it's important to note that we're still not working at the final size of the animation. In fact, it's best to work at a minimum of twice the size of the final animation to ensure a quality result.

Introducing the Background Texture and Global Lighting

Now that the image has been reduced to the working resolution, we're ready to begin working on a texture for the background. In this case, we'll create a background that has a brushed metal appearance. In order to produce this appearance, we'll rely on the Motion Blur filter, which unfortunately produces unwanted edge effects. Therefore, we'll have to temporarily enlarge the canvas so that these edge effects are clipped when the canvas is reduced back to its original size.

But this is just the beginning. Once the brushed metal texture has been introduced, we'll then implement some additional steps to produce a more three-dimensional appearance by introducing recessed regions around the gears using the Lighting Effects filter in conjunction with some specially defined channels. Finally, we'll introduce a gradient to enhance the global lighting of the image before proceeding to prepare the gears to be animated. Let's get started!

As already mentioned, the Motion Blur filter has generated some unwanted edge effects, but we'll wait until we've completed the background before resizing the image back to its original size.

I Choose Image➡Canvas Size and then specify the settings as shown. Now choose View➡Fit on Screen. Set the foreground color to green (R:90 G:155 B:120) and then fill the layer with the foreground color. Now choose Filter➡Noise➡Add Noise (Amount: 100, Distribution: Uniform, Monochromatic: unchecked) and then choose Filter➡Blur➡Motion Blur (Angle:0 degrees, Distance: 100 pixels).

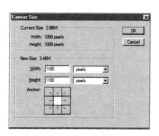

2 With the Elliptical Marquee tool selected, place the cursor at pixel location (117,212) and then drag out a circular selection to (669,765). Hold the Shift key and drag out another selection from (589,188) to (980,578) in order to add it to the current selection. Now choose Select➡Modify➡Smooth (16 pixels) to smooth out the points where the two selections join.

Now save the selection to a new channel (Channel #4) and then deselect the selection. Make Channel #4 active and then choose Filter➥Blur➥Gaussian Blur (Radius: 4.0 pixels).

At this point, the resulting background looks great. The addition of the recessed region will really help to enhance the appearance of the final image. It's also important to note that the Lighting Effects filter simply adds shadows and highlights to the regions where transitions existed in the mask of Channel #4. In other words, the apparent depth of the recessed region was determined by the radius of the Gaussian Blur that was applied to the channel in the previous step. In fact, the recessed region would not have even been produced without first applying the blur filter as we did.

Before proceeding, make the RGB channel active once again. In the next step, we'll use this mask with the Lighting Effects filter to create a recessed region that surrounds Gear1a and Gear2.

3 With the Background layer still active, choose Filter➡Render➡Lighting effects and adjust the settings as shown. Most importantly, specify Channel #4 in the Texture Channel field and then turn off the White is high option. Before applying, adjust the light source in the preview window so that it is placed in the upper-left corner at approximately 45 degrees. Now delete Channel #4, which is no longer needed.

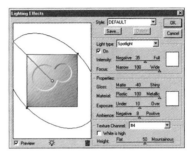

4 Make the Gear3.eps layer active and then create a new layer named Global Light. Select the gradient tool from the toolbox. In the Gradient Tool Options Palette, reset the tool and then choose Cancel when prompted. Specify Transparent to Foreground in the Gradient field. Now switch to the default colors and then drag out a gradient from the extreme upper left to the extreme lower right extents of the image window. Adjust the layer opacity to 35%.

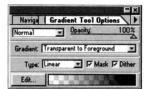

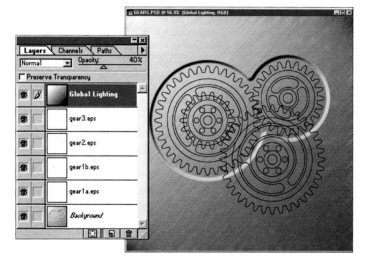

5 Now that the background texture is complete, we'll go ahead and resize it back to its original size. Before proceeding, choose Image➡Canvas Size and specify the settings as shown and then choose Proceed when prompted. We'll now move on to complete the gears.

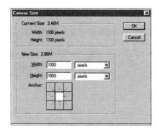

GEARS.PSD @ 62.6% (Global Lighting, RGB)

Setting Up Gear3

Before we proceed, it's important to note that the remaining operations of this chapter will not explicitly instruct you on how to implement all of the operations that are necessary to complete every gear of the system. Instead, the ensuing steps of this section and the next will specifically describe how to set up and animate Gear3. Once we've completed these two sections, you'll then possess all the knowledge that is required to set up the basic elements and update the action to include the remaining gears as well. Nevertheless, it's also important to note you won't be required to perform these additional operations because the CD-ROM provides you with all the working files that I used to complete the GIF animation which appears on the CD-ROM as well.

In this section, we'll concentrate on the development of several basic components that will be required by the action to create the final appearance of Gear3 for each frame of the animation. More specifically, we'll create the basic texture for the gear as well as two channels that will then be used by the action to create a more three-dimensional appearance for the gears in exactly the same way that we introduced the recessed regions in the background using the Lighting Effects filter.

As a result of the approach that we'll be following, it's important to note that you won't actually see the final appearance of the gear until we've completed the operations of the next section. In fact, we'll proceed through the operations of this section with little explanation because the exact purpose of the elements that we'll be producing will become clear when we actually use them as we write the action. We'll now get started by first developing the gear texture before we produce the two channels.

1 Make the Gear3.eps layer active and then make the other EPS layers invisible. Now create a new layer named G3 Body. Using the Rectangular Marquee tool, drag out a selection from (383,344) to (935,898). Now set the foreground color to gold (R:255 G:175 B:0) and then fill the layer with the foreground color.

Choose Filter➞Noise➞Add Noise (Amount: 100, Distribution: Uniform, Monochromatic: Unchecked) and then select Filter➞Blur➞Radial Blur (Amount: 20, Method: Spin, Quality: Best).

Now Choose Image➞Adjust➞Brightness/Contrast Brightness: 20, Contrast: 40). Deselect the selection.

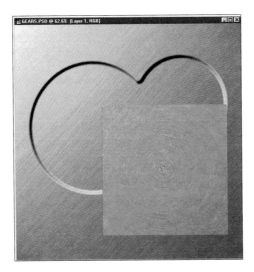

At this point, it's important to note that several minutes will be required by your system (even on a fast computer) to work through the necessary calculations of the Radial Blur filter in the Best quality mode. Nevertheless, don't be tempted to apply the filter in one of the lower quality modes because the resulting texture will not produce an appearance that is realistic in the final animation. You also shouldn't be surprised by the resulting texture that is produced by the Best quality mode since the appearance of this texture will improve dramatically when the Lighting Effects filter is applied in the next section. Remember to be patient while the filter is running. So now's a good time to take a five-minute break while your computer chugs through the necessary calculations.

2 In the Layers palette, move the G3 Body layer below the Gear3.eps layer and then use the Move tool to center the texture under the outline of the gear if necessary. Now make the Gear3.eps layer active. With the Magic Wand tool selected, hold the Shift key and select the perimeter region as well as the three

cutout regions between the spokes of the gear as indicated in the accompanying figure.

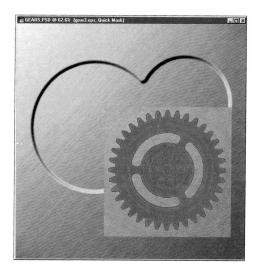

Choose Select➡Modify➡Expand (1 pixel) and then make the G3 Body layer active once again. Now press the Delete key to remove the selected regions and then deselect the selection.

3 Make the Gear3.eps layer active. With the Magic Wand tool still selected, hold the Shift key and select the two regions of the gear as indicated in the accompanying figure.

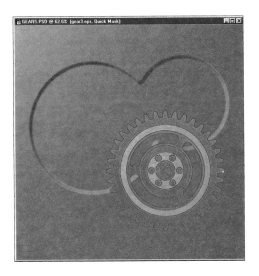

Now choose Select➡Expand (1 pixel). Make the G3 Body layer active and then choose Image➡Adjust➡Hue/Saturation (Hue: -180, Saturation: -51, Lightness: -67). Deselect the selection.

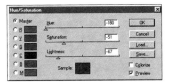

Let's now move on to create and edit the two channels. As already mentioned, these channels will be used to create a 3-D appearance for the gear. In fact, we'll use them in conjunction with the Lighting Effects filter in exactly the same way that we did to produce the recessed region of the background texture in Step 3 of the previous section. You'll probably remember that the characteristics of the recessed edges were dependent on the blurring operation that was applied to the channel before the Lighting Effects filter was applied to the texture, and things are no different here.

4 Make the Gear3.eps layer active. Using the Magic Wand tool, hold the Shift key and select the outermost region as well as the spoked region of the gear as indicated in the accompanying figure.

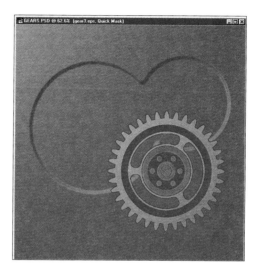

Save the selection to a new channel named Gear3-1. Now make the Gear3-1 channel active and then deselect the selection. With the Magic Wand tool still selected, place the cursor at pixel location (650,620) to select the central black region and then choose Select➡Modify➡Expand (2 pixels). Now switch to the default colors and then fill the selection with the foreground color. Deselect the selection. In the next step, we'll implement a few more editing operations to complete this mask.

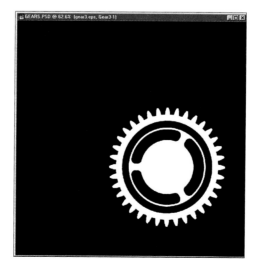

5 Using the Elliptical Marquee tool, place the cursor at pixel location (445,410) and drag out a selection to (869,834). Choose Filter➥Blur➥Gaussian Blur (Radius: 2.0 pixels). Now invert the selection and then choose Filter➥Blur➥Gaussian Blur (Radius: 1.0 pixels) to blur the edges of the teeth. Before proceeding, deselect the selection and then make the RGB channel active. Let's move on to create the second channel.

In this case, we used the selection to blur the outer perimeter of the gear mask by a smaller amount than the interior edges. This will produce sharper edges for the gear teeth in the final appearance of the gear. This will become more clear when we use the channel in the next section.

6 With the Gear3.eps layer still active, hold the Shift key and select the six buttons and the two adjacent ringed regions as indicated in the accompanying image.

Now save the selection to a new channel named Gear3-2 and then deselect the selection. In the channels palette, make the selection active and then choose Filter➡Blur➡Gaussian Blur (Radius: 2.0 pixels).

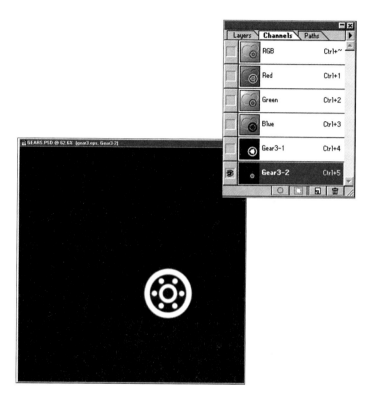

In this case, we'll keep the Outline layer separate from the G3 Body layer to ensure that it's appearance is not altered by the Lighting Effects filter, which we'll be applying to the G3 Body layer in the next section. However, by linking the two layers, the outline layer will be rotated automatically whenever the G3 Body layer is rotated. In fact, it's important to note that this feature is very convenient because both layers will have to be rotated between each frame of the animation.

Now that the channels are both in place, we'll move on to modify the outline to make it look smoother and darker. Then we'll begin to write the action to animate the gear, but before proceeding, make the RGB channel active.

7 With the Gear3.eps layer still active, choose Filter➡Blur (Radius: 0.5 pixels). Duplicate the Gear3.eps layer and then merge down the duplicate layer (Gear3.eps copy) with the Gear3.eps layer. At this point, the outline should look smoother and darker. Now link the Gear3.eps layer with the G3 Body layer.

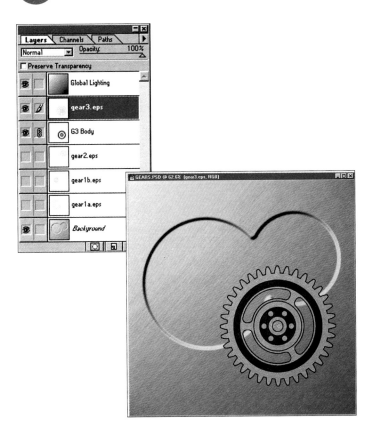

Writing the Action

Now we're ready to write the action to produce the individual frames of the animation. But first we must implement a little bit of math to figure out some basic parameters so that we can then write the action to produce an animation that plays back smoothly after it's been created. In fact, we'll start by calculating a suitable rotation rate for the gear.

When animating the gear, it's important that the gear be rotated by less than half the angular coverage of a single tooth. As we proceed, keep in mind that there are 360 degrees in a circle. In this case, Gear3 has 36 teeth so that the angular coverage of each tooth is 10 degrees (360 degrees/36 teeth). Therefore, the gear must be rotated by less than 5 degrees (10 degrees / 2) between each animation frame that is generated. In fact, we'll write the action to rotate the gear by 4.0 degrees between each frame. This means that 90 frames (360 degrees/4 degrees per frame) will be required to produce a complete rotation of the gear. The gear, however, is symmetrical every 120 degrees so that the appearance of continuous rotation can be produced with only 30 frames (120 degrees/4 degrees per frame).

Now that we know the general parameters of the animation, we can proceed to write the specific steps of the action. In this case, we'll define the action to incrementally rotate the gear body, outline, and associated channels between each frame that is to be generated. Each time the action rotates these elements, it will also be defined to make a duplicate of the gear body and apply the Lighting Effects filter to the duplicate with each of the two channels to produce a three-dimensional appearance for the gear. The action will then create a layer drop shadow before saving the animation frame. Once the frame has been saved, the action will then discard the duplicate layer as well as the layer drop shadow before repeating all of these operations to create the next frame as well.

I saved a copy of my own working file that is provided on the CD-ROM for your convenience as GEAR.PSD. The CD-ROM also contains a copy of the action that I defined by following the ensuing steps of this section. This action is provided on the CD-ROM as GEAR.ATN. Feel free to reference these files as you see fit.

1 Before proceeding, save a copy of your working file. Choose File➡Save a Copy and then save the file as GEARS.PSD.

2 If the Actions palette is not currently open, choose Window➡Show Actions. Now select the New Action command from the Actions palette pullout menu. In the dialog box that appears, name the action GEARS.ATN. The action is now in record mode as indicated by the red circle at the bottom of the palette.

As we proceed, you'll notice that Photoshop will add a new command to the action for each command we implement. Therefore, you need to take your time to be careful and follow the ensuing instructions explicitly if you are not already familiar with this capability.

Let's move on to record the first commands of our action. In this case, the first several commands that we'll record will be transformations to rotate the G3 Body layer as well as the two channels. As already mentioned, the Gear3.eps layer will automatically be rotated since it is linked to the G3 Body layer.

3 Make the G3 Body layer active and then choose
Layer➡Transform➡Numeric. In the dialog box that appears,
specify a rotation angle of 4.0 degrees and then disable all the
other input fields before applying.

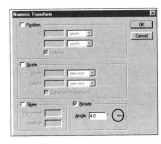 

At this point, both the G3 Body layer and the Gear3.eps layer
have been rotated and the action has recorded two commands.
Not only did it record the transformation, but it also recorded
the selection of the G3 Body layer. To see this more clearly, let's
stop recording our action for just a moment to check things out
in more detail.

4 Choose the Stop Recording command from the actions palette
pullout menu. Now click the arrows for each of the two commands that are displayed so that the details of each command
become visible.

Make sure not to click anything else so that you don't alter the
current state of the action. Most importantly, we want the
Transform command to remain active so that the action will start
recording from where it left off when we proceed.

At this point, notice that the Select command specifies the layer
that was selected and the Transform command specifies the exact
transform that was applied.

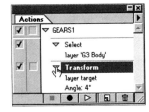

Now let's begin recording again. Before proceeding, click the
arrows to hide the details of each command. With the Transform
command still active, choose the Start Recording command from
the palette pullout menu so that the action is now back in the

recording mode once again. We'll now move on to rotate the channels using the same numeric transform that we used in the previous step.

5 In the Channels palette, make the Gear3-1 channel active and then choose Layer➥Transform➥Numeric again. Apply the transform without altering the current settings. Now make the Gear3-2 channel active and then choose Layer➥Transform➥ Numeric. Once again, apply the transform without altering the current settings.

At this point, all the relevant layers and channels have been rotated, and we're now ready to apply the Lighting Effects filter to the gear to produce the three-dimensional appearance that we seek. In this case, we'll actually have to apply the Lighting Effects filter twice (once with each channel), but before we proceed to apply this filter, there are a few things you need to know.

Most importantly, you need to know that the action will not record the individual settings of the Lighting Effects filter. As a result, the action will prompt you during playback to define new settings each time the filter is to be applied, which is a major hassle. Nevertheless, the filter does retain the settings with which it was last applied. In fact, we can actually use this characteristic to simplify user interaction during playback by defining default settings that we can simply accept each and every time the filter is applied.

However, if we simply accept the default settings of the filter each time it is used (as desired to simplify user interaction during playback), we won't be able to switch between the two channels as required, but there is a way to get around this limitation by first defining a third channel named TEMP HOLD and then defining the action to copy other channels to the TEMP HOLD channel as they are needed. This way, the Lighting Effects filter can be defined to consistently access the TEMP HOLD channel so that there is no need to alter the default settings of the filter whenever it is applied. This will become more clear as we implement the ensuing steps.

6 Choose the Stop Recording command from the Actions palette pullout menu. In the channels palette, create a new channel named TEMP HOLD and then choose the Start Recording command from the Actions palette pullout menu. Now make the Gear3-1 channel active. Choose Select➡All and then choose Edit➡Copy to copy the channel to the clipboard. Now deselect the selection. Then make the TEMP HOLD channel active and choose Edit➡Paste to paste the contents of the clipboard to the TEMP HOLD channel. Now make the RGB channel active before returning to the Layers palette.

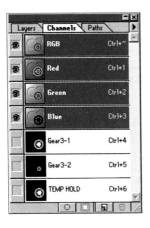

7 Duplicate the G3 Body layer. With the duplicate layer (G3 Body copy) now active, choose Filter➡Render➡Lighting Effects and then adjust the settings as shown. Most importantly, specify TEMP HOLD as the Texture channel. Also, turn on the White is high option and then adjust the lighting parameters in the preview window as shown. Before proceeding, click the Save button at the top of the dialog box and save the settings to Gears before applying the filter.

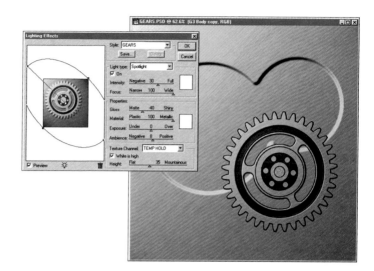

In this case, the Lighting Effects filter was used only to introduce additional highlights to produce a more three-dimensional appearance for a very localized region of the gear. We need to be careful, however, when applying the filter more than once, since additional applications with the settings that we're using will tend to darken the overall appearance of the existing texture. This is why we used the selection to limit the effect of the filter to the local region where the highlights were introduced. Although this region is now darkened, the change in brightness actually looks quite acceptable. In other words, it's reasonable to expect that there would be some brightness variations across the surface of a brushed metal gear, and we've actually introduced these variations without changing the overall brightness that was achieved with the first application of the filter.

8 In the Channels palette, make the Gear3-2 channel active. Choose Select➡All and then use the selection to copy the channel mask to the clipboard. Make the TEMP HOLD channel active and then choose Edit➡Paste to place the contents of the clipboard to the channel and then deselect the selection. Now load the selection from the TEMP HOLD channel as well. Choose Select➡Modify➡Expand (2 pixels) and then make the RGB channel active. With the duplicate layer (G3 Body copy) still active, choose Filter➡Render➡Lighting Effects once again. Apply the filter without changing any of the settings and then deselect the selection.

9 Now we'll create a layer drop shadow to enhance the three dimensional character of the gear even further. Make the G3 Body layer active and then load the layer transparency selection from the layer as well. Now create a layer drop shadow named Shadow and then choose Select➡Feather (Radius: 4.0 pixels). Deselect the selection. We're now ready to generate the first frame.

10 Choose Image➡Duplicate. In the dialog box that now appears, specify Frame as the name and then turn on the Merged Layers Only option. With the duplicate image now active, choose Image➡Image Size and specify new pixel dimensions of 300 × 300. Now choose View➡Fit on Screen and then choose View➡Actual Pixels to display the frame at its native resolution of 72 dpi.

It's important to note that View commands are not recorded by actions. Therefore, you will not see the remaining frames at the native resolution when you play the action. The duplicate image is now ready to be exported.

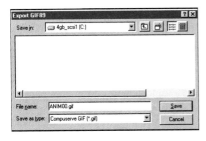

11 Choose File➡Export➡GIF89a Export. In the dialog box that now appears, specify the settings as shown. In the next dialog box that appears, specify ANIM00.GIF as the name and then save the file. Now close the duplicate image (FRAME).

12 In the Layers palette, delete the Shadow layer and then delete the duplicate layer (G3 Body copy). Now choose the Stop Recording command from the Actions palette pullout menu. At this point, the action is essentially complete, but there is one last thing that must done before you can play back the action to generate the remaining frames. In the Actions palette, toggle on the dialog box in front of the export command. This tells the action to prompt you with a dialog box so that you can specify a different filename for each new frame before it is exported. Also, keep in mind that you'll have to click the Play button each time you want to generate another frame.

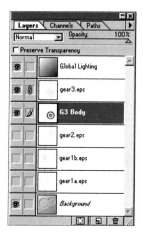

Determining the Rotation Rates for the Remaining Gears

At this point, you have all the information that is required to complete the remaining gears with one exception. You also need the rotation angles for the remaining gears since each gear will have its own rate of rotation. These angles are provided in the table below and were all calculated using the following equation which relates the number of teeth and rotation angles of inter-meshing gears:

$$Na \times Aa = -(Nb \times Ab)$$

where:

Na	= Number of Teeth for Gear a
Aa	= Angle/Frame for Gear a
Nb	= Number of Teeth for Gear b
Ab	= Angle/Frame for Gear b

It's important to note that the rotation rate of each gear was determined to be less than half the angular coverage for a single tooth of that gear so that all gears in the system will appear to rotate smoothly. Remember,

Angular Coverage per Tooth = (360 degrees)/(Number of Teeth)

Gear Number	Number of Teeth	Angle per Frame	Angular Coverage per Tooth
1a	36	+ 4.0 degrees	10.0 degrees
1b	18	+ 4.0 degrees	20 degrees
2	24	- 6.0 degrees	15 degrees
3	36	- 2.0 degrees	10 degrees

Playing the Action and Generating the Frames

Let's begin to explore the working files on the CD-ROM. Before loading these files, it's recommended that you save and close your own working file for the time being. Once you've completed this section and studied the working file as well as the action of the CD-ROM in more detail, you'll then be in a better position to complete your own working file and action if you wish to do so.

Note that you do not have to complete the remaining gears because the CD-ROM contains the working files that I used to generate the frames of the GIF

continues

continued

animation that also appear on the CD-ROM. More specifically, this section will describe how you can use the SYSTEM.PSD file in conjunction with the actions stored in the SYSTEM.ATN file to produce the final GIF animation that appears on the CD-ROM as SYSTEM.GIF. An AVI formatted version of the animation also appears on the CD-ROM as SYSTEM.AVI.

I Open the file named SYSTEM.PSD. This file contains the basic components that are required by the action to generate the final animation.

2 We'll now load the action. In the Actions palette, choose the Load Action command from the palette pullout menu to open the file named SYSTEM.ATN. Several new actions will be added to the palette as shown in the accompanying image.

3 Now make the action named Make 60 Frames active and then choose the Play Action command from the palette pullout menu as well. When the Lighting Effects dialog box appears for the first time, specify the settings as shown in the accompanying image. Once you've defined these settings, you won't have to change them again. Simply press the Enter key to accept the default settings each time the Lighting Effects dialog box reappears until all 60 frames have been generated. You'll also be prompted to specify a filename for each frame before it is saved. Make sure to name each frame successively (Frame00.gif, Frame01.gif,...,Frame59.gif, and so on).

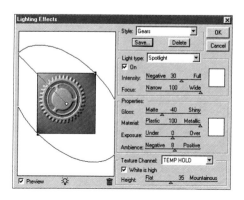

Assembling the Frames

At this point, Photoshop is no longer required because it cannot assemble the frames into the final animation. This requires the use of a third-party application and plenty of freeware and shareware applications are readily available that can even be pulled off the Internet. Two of the more popular software applications include the GIF Construction Set for use in Windows and the GIF Builder for the Mac. Each of these applications is incredibly simple and easy to learn. Therefore, I won't cover the specific operations that are required to use them.

In addition to these applications, other excellent commercial products can also be used to increase the quality of your final animation. In fact, I don't recommend that you export to the GIF format directly from Photoshop because this format is not a full-color format. As a result, Photoshop exports the frames individually so that they are not globally optimized. Instead, my preference is to save the individual frames to a full-color format (such as TIF or TGA). I then use DeBabelizer to determine an optimized, global palette that is Netscape-compatible based on the full-color images to produce a higher quality result.

In fact, the CD-ROM provides all 60 of the animation frames as true color images in the TIF format which you can readily use to assemble a true color animation of your own. These frames were generated with the working file and the actions described in the previous section. Even though the CD-ROM does not provide the frames in the GIF format, keep in mind that you can easily open the TIF files in Photoshop to export them to this format as well as others that are compatible with the capabilities of the frame assembler that you prefer to use.

Using the Extra Gears

Although the majority of you probably don't have access to the Advanced Modeling Extension of AutoCAD R12, I've provided several additional gear outlines of various sizes that you can use to define your own gear systems outside the scope of this technique. It's important to note that all the gears are completely consistent. In other words, they all have the same pitch and scale so that each individual gear will properly mesh with the other gears that are provided. In fact, the nominal diameter of each gear can be determined by dividing its number of teeth by 10. In other words, the gears with 18 teeth have nominal diameters of 1.8 inches whereas the gears with 36 teeth have nominal diameters of 3.6 inches.

When importing the gears into Photoshop, it's important to note that the Place command will introduce each gear with the correct physical dimensions regardless of the resolution of the file. Therefore, you'll want to define the absolute size of your working image based on a consideration of the size, number, and positions of the gears that you'll be introducing. Keep in mind that the resolution setting only affects the quality of the image and has no effect on the default sizes that the gears will automatically assume when they are placed. Also, it's important to know that the Place command will automatically center each gear within the image window so that you can always determine the initial position of the gear based on the size of the image.

Nevertheless, some care must be exercised when importing and manipulating gears in Photoshop. When using the Place command to import EPS files, for example, it's best to maximize the view of the image window and then leave it alone until all the gears are introduced. When placing a gear, it's also best to accept the initial default size and position of the gear. You can then transform it from its original state once the placement has been completed.

Keep in mind that you cannot scale an individual gear without scaling all other gears by exactly the same amount if you want them to properly mesh. Therefore, it's best to implement all scaling transformations numerically. You'll achieve the best results when you plan things out carefully and accurately, which is especially true when producing images and, more importantly, complex animations.

Index

Symbols

A

F

G

MACMILLAN COMPUTER PUBLISHING USA

A VIACOM COMPANY

Technical

Support:

If you need assistance with the information in this book or with a CD/Disk accompanying the book, please access the Knowledge Base on our Web site at **http://www.superlibrary.com/general/support**. Our most Frequently Asked Questions are answered there. If you do not find the answer to your questions on our Web site, you may contact Macmillan Technical Support **(317) 581-3833** or e-mail us at **support@mcp.com**.

What's on the CD-ROM?

■ GIF Construction Set for Windows (3.1 and 95/NT) from Alchemy MindWorks: a powerful graphics tool that helps you to create new or modify existing GIF files into interlaced, animated, or transparent format all through the use of its Animation Wizard tool.

The GIF Construction Set software included with this publication is provided as shareware for your evaluation. If you try this software and find it useful, you are requested to register it as discussed in its documenation and in the About screen of the application. The publisher of this book has not paid the registration fee for this shareware but has been granted permission to distribute said software.

■ GIFbuilder: a scriptable free Mac utility for creating animated GIF files.

■ Numerous GIF and TIFF images highlighted as examples throughout the book made available to both Windows and Mac users.